"During my career I have had the opportunity to work with many exceptionally talented individuals—all of whom, to a varying degree, have practiced some of what Shundrawn Thomas offers in this groundbreaking book. After reading *Discover Joy in Work* all of our views on work and the workplace will be significantly changed."

Samuel C. Scott III, former president and chief executive officer,
Corn Products, board director for Abbott Laboratories, Bank of New York Mellon and Motorola Solutions Inc.

"From the very beginning work has been a significant part of our human experience. And thankfully we are wired for it. Adam was built to work the garden and steward its beauty. But like everything else in life, managing what we are built for can be a challenging task in and of itself. So for all of us who are tempted to think that work is a necessary evil . . . we desperately need to read Shundrawn Thomas's revolutionary thoughts about how to turn our work from drudgery to joy!"

Joe Stowell, president, Cornerstone University

"With *Discover Joy in Work*, Shundrawn Thomas combines profound insights, practical experience, and vivid anecdotes to produce a road map for those seeking greater fulfillment in their work. This book is a must-read for anyone seeking to grow professionally and personally."

Leslie D. Hale, president and chief executive officer, RLJ Lodging Trust

"Most of us will spend much of our waking hours in our work environment. Few of us have reflected on how our work can be joyful. The author of this book was able to find joy in his work and transform his occupation into his vocation. As a result, he grew into the person he was becoming and in his contributions to those he worked with and those he served. *Discover Joy in Work* will open new opportunities for work to become a pathway to joy in your life."

C. William Pollard, former chief executive officer, The ServiceMaster Company, and author of *The Soul of the Firm*

"Shundrawn Thomas is a shining example of the power of merging purpose and profession to the glory of God. *Discover Joy in Work* is a timely invitation to experience God's best in your daily work."

Nicholas Pearce, professor at Northwestern University, assistant pastor of Apostolic Church of God, author of *The Purpose Path*

"With *Discover Joy in Work*, Shundrawn brings an insightful and unique perspective to the age-old question of how we find joy in the work that we do every day. His book is a practical guide to the steps anyone can take to create a more fulfilling career journey and to love what they do."

Lisa Warner Wardell, president and chief executive officer, Adtalem Global Education

"Shundrawn Thomas has written a remarkable book, a work full of cosmic wisdom and concrete advice for anybody seeking to live a life of greater joy, fulfillment, and service. By highlighting the ways our work lives might be improved, Shundrawn shows us a path where our whole selves can be enriched. I highly recommend this book."

Eboo Patel, author of *Acts of Faith*, president of Interfaith Youth Core

"Transformed! That is the best word to describe your mindset after reading *Discover Joy in Work*. Shundrawn Thomas's ability to seamlessly weave together timely research, piercing insights, and vivid storytelling provides a truly unique perspective on work as a calling. Reader beware! This book will impact you intellectually, emotionally, and spiritually, encouraging your growth in the process."

Carla A. Harris, vice chairman of wealth management, Morgan Stanley, author of *Expect to Win*

"Shundrawn Thomas delivers a prophetic message to this generation and generations to come. In *Discover Joy in Work*, his keen insight and principled character shine through as he inspires the novice and the elder to realize their true vocation and higher calling."

Emery Lindsey, presiding bishop of the Western Diocese, pastor of Christ Temple Cathedral

"Throughout my career as a scientist, administrator, and educator, I have had the privilege of mentoring talented professionals and brilliant students. I can personally attest that one of the greatest needs of professionals and students alike is wise career counsel. Shundrawn Thomas provides this oft sought-after wisdom and so much more. Whether you are just beginning your career journey or are well along the path, *Discover Joy in Work* offers the unique insights, inspirational guidance, and practical applications that will help you flourish professionally, personally, and spiritually."

Larry Robinson, president of Florida A&M University

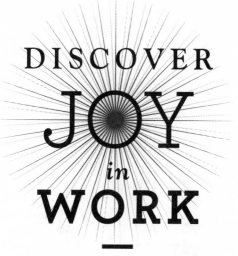

DISCOVER JOY in WORK

TRANSFORMING YOUR OCCUPATION INTO YOUR VOCATION

SHUNDRAWN A. THOMAS

An imprint of InterVarsity Press
Downers Grove, Illinois

InterVarsity Press
P.O. Box 1400, Downers Grove, IL 60515-1426
ivpress.com
email@ivpress.com

InterVarsity Press® is the book-publishing division of InterVarsity Christian Fellowship/USA®, a movement of
students and faculty active on campus at hundreds of universities, colleges, and schools of nursing in the
United States of America, and a member movement of the International Fellowship of Evangelical Students.
For information about local and regional activities, visit intervarsity.org.

All Scripture quotations, unless otherwise indicated, are taken from The Holy Bible, New International
Version®, NIV®. Copyright © 1973, 1978, 1984, 2011 by Biblica, Inc.™ Used by permission of
Zondervan. All rights reserved worldwide. www.zondervan.com. The "NIV" and "New International
Version" are trademarks registered in the United States Patent and Trademark Office by Biblica, Inc.™

While any stories in this book are true, some names and identifying information may have been changed to
protect the privacy of individuals.

Cover design and image composite: David Fassett
Interior design: Daniel van Loon
Images: stars: © Shin Tukinaga / Moment / Getty Images
        flowing water: © greenantphoto / iStock / Getty Images Plus

ISBN 978-0-8308-4574-3 (print)
ISBN 978-0-8308-5798-2 (digital)

Printed in the United States of America ♾

InterVarsity Press is committed to ecological stewardship and to the conservation of natural resources in all
our operations. This book was printed using sustainably sourced paper.

Library of Congress Cataloging-in-Publication Data
A catalog record for this book is available from the Library of Congress.

P	22	21	20	19	18	17	16	15	14	13	12	11	10	9	8	7	6	5	4	3	2	1
Y	39	38	37	36	35	34	33	32	31	30	29	28	27	26	25	24	23	22	21	20	19

This book is dedicated
to the working world.

CONTENTS

PREFACE

WORK AND HAPPINESS

Men for the sake of getting a living forget to live.

Margaret Fuller

Years ago, I was invited to a dinner meeting with a small group of accomplished professionals. This turned out to be the inaugural meeting of a group that would gather for years to come. Among the group of twelve were several corporate executives, several partners from law firms, two leaders in the nonprofit sector, a private equity investor, and an entrepreneur. The group coalesced around the concept of encouraging one another in our personal and professional development. While the members of the group were loosely connected through mutual relationships, the first step on our journey was simply getting acquainted with one another.

We began by sharing basic personal information about our families and ourselves. We then, in a more structured manner, discussed our career experience, current responsibilities, and future aspirations. The final speaker took a very different approach. Raymond was an accomplished artist and a director at a nonprofit organization. Prior to discussing his professional experience and career aspirations, he posed a question to the group. "Are you happy?" he asked. The words seemed to suspend in silence over the group. "Are you happy?" he repeated. The simple yet profound question changed the entire tenor of the dialogue.

As the final contributor, Raymond had the unique perspective of hearing from all the other participants. He said he was impressed with the collective experiences and achievements of the group. While it was clear the group was composed of individuals with pedigrees of professional success, it was not altogether clear the individuals found lasting fulfillment in their work. Happiness and work—it seems—are strange bedfellows. It was natural for the members to pursue and expect success in their professional pursuits. It was, however, foreign for this same group to seek or expect happiness in their professional experience. Apparently, happiness in work or the workplace is a bonus, not an expectation.

It turns out the question was not only profound but was in some ways prophetic. Over the course of the next two years, half of the group pursued new career opportunities. In each instance, the individual elected to leave a situation where they had enjoyed notable success and reasonably long tenures. Some pursued opportunities more in line with their personal passions while others pursued better career opportunities or entrepreneurial endeavors. While it was never explicitly stated, each move in some way reflected a desire to achieve more professional fulfillment and achievement. What about happiness? Is there joy in work?

The members of our group continue to meet periodically to promote personal and professional development. Those who have made career transitions seem to be faring well professionally. Some or all of these professional transitions may prove beneficial in the long run. However, these career moves alone will not bring more joy. Those who changed jobs testify to the fact they generally found identical or similar challenges in their new workplaces. Our personal experiences revealed a great truth. Joy is something we only find through introspective search. The search for joy in work is more about our attitude and less about our environment.

The greatest inhibitor to experiencing joy in our work is the attitude and actions of the man or woman in the mirror. Where we work is an important question to be sure. Given a choice, one should choose wisely. How we choose to perform our work is, however, the more essential question. Setting aside the human tendency toward self-centeredness is a prerequisite to discovering joy in our work. This requires us to rise above selfish ambition. It also requires us to mature mentally and spiritually, so our true motivation originates from our inner being.

I made an important decision during that first dinner meeting. I decided to transform my occupation into my vocation. This entails daily taking individual accountability for growing personally and professionally. This has been my path to discovering joy in my work. This personal revelation inspired me to write this book. I pray it encourages you to truly *live* as you *get a living*. I pray you will similarly transform your occupation into your vocation, and by doing so, find joy in your work.

INTRODUCTION

NO JOY IN MUDVILLE

We are at our very best, and are happiest, when we are fully
engaged in work we enjoy on the journey toward the goal
we established for ourselves. It gives meaning to our time
off and comfort to our sleep. It makes everything
else in life so wonderful, so worthwhile.

EARL NIGHTINGALE

The world has an employee engagement crisis, with serious and potentially lasting repercussions for the global economy."[1] This was the lead to an article published by Gallup, Inc., a preeminent research and consulting company with a stated mission to help leaders and organizations solve their most pressing problems. The company focuses on several key practice areas including "talent management" and "employee engagement." In short, they can help solve people problems. Gallup characterizes *engaged* employees as those who are enthusiastic about their work and committed to their work and workplace. Gallup has been tracking employee engagement since 2000 with sobering results. According to Gallup, less than one-third of US employees are engaged, with only 13 percent of employees engaged worldwide.

Organizations of all shapes and sizes experience this general lack of engagement. It is a particularly acute problem given the intensive efforts to improve engagement over the last decade.

What does employee engagement have to do with joy in work? From the perspective of the organization, engaged employees take positive actions to further the mission of the organization, which improves performance metrics and enhances the organization's reputation. From the perspective of the individual, *engaged employees* are physically, intellectually, and emotionally committed to their work. It can be said they bring their whole selves to their work. While they value tangible and intangible forms of compensation, they are motivated less by pay and more by purpose. Engaged employees at all levels are the true drivers of an organization's long-term success. I believe engaged employees are likely individuals who find meaning and, yes, joy in their work. The outcome of engagement is mutually beneficial for the organization and the individual, aligning organizational mission with personal fulfillment.

IT'S NOT JUST A JOB

One of my more telling qualities is I am exacting about words. This is partly due to my temperament and more so due to my calling. I have intentionally chosen to use the term *work* as the first of several key words that undergird the central theme of the book. I have also intentionally avoided the term *job*, which is often used as a surrogate. While the words are commonly treated as interchangeable, they have different etymologies and connotations. Anecdotally, I have observed the terms are often used differently expressing different emotions and viewpoints. Henri Nouwen revealed a great truth when he observed "the greatest joy as well as the greatest pain of living come not only from what we live but even more from how we think and feel about what we are living."[2] Words have incredible power, shaping the way we define our world and how we experience it. Let's consider the meaning of each word and the attitudes each evokes.

The term *job* is defined as a duty or chore, which implies an obligatory undertaking. We generally associate it with something a person does regularly to earn money. The derivation of the word is quite insightful. The origin, roughly defined, signifies a task or piece of work done for pay and generally referred to petty or piddling work. I think this in many respects is profound because it closely aligns with many people's perspective of their job. People generally associate a job with activity or busyness. It is usually linked to wages. A job is often viewed as a burden to be borne. A job is assigned by others as opposed to developed by the individual. People thank God for Friday for many unspoken reasons that reflect attitudes about and experiences related to their jobs. The term *job* also has a direct association with the term *occupation*. While the term *occupation* refers to one's profession, the basic definition is any activity that takes up time and earns money. An occupation may be an activity that brings one pleasure, but principally, it simply needs to be done.

The term *work* is defined as mental or physical effort done to achieve an intended result. The effort is often part of a larger undertaking or mission. We generally associate work with productivity. The derivation of the word is equally insightful. The origin means to perform, make, construct, or produce. It is related to a skilled trade or craft. This in many respects mirrors how individuals view their work. Ideas generated, products made, and services rendered are not simply for barter or sale. People identify themselves with their occupation and can easily immerse themselves in their work. Work is in part about making a living. However, our work reflects our passions and purpose. Moreover, there is value in the work process and the work product. Work can be personalized and at the same time is part of a greater good or mission.

The term *work* has a direct relationship to the term *vocation*. The term *vocation* is derived from a Latin term that means "call" or "summons." A vocation refers to work you feel especially suited for and is worthy of great dedication. Your choice of vocation is one for which you have a deep affinity and which offers enjoyment.

If we consider the terms as defined, it becomes plain to see how the words suggest different attitudes. When we consider an effort viewed as a chore at best and a burden at worst, it is likely to engender apathy. If we can only see the task at hand as opposed to the vision ahead, it becomes plain to see how people become disengaged. If wages are our primary incentive, the task will occupy our hands but never capture our hearts. Conversely, if work cultivates skill and ability, it offers physical, emotional, and spiritual value that far exceeds remuneration. If we are passionate about our work, we more readily develop a sense of calling. Our occupation can become our vocation. This, however, is a function of how we view our work. If we see ourselves as serving the human community, we are well on the path to discovering joy in our work.

JOYFUL WORK

In the same vein of being exacting in the use of language, here is another word essential to the theme of this book—*joy*. Joy is a source or cause of great happiness or pleasure. Joy may be evoked by triumph, discovery, or attainment of something exceptionally good. While joy stirs our emotions, it is more than a feeling. A calm and contentment accompanies this emotional state. True joy does not emanate from external conditions or our emotional state. True joy is an attitude of the heart that informs our way of thinking and feeling. Karl Barth may have captured it best when he remarked, "Joy is the simplest form of gratitude."[3] I find gratefulness often accompanied by joyfulness.

My guess is joy is not the first word that comes to mind when most people think of work. Many view happiness and work as strange bedfellows. I recall a time in my career when I confided to a mentor I wasn't truly happy or fulfilled in my work. He replied bluntly, "That's why they call it work." This brought to mind a memorable stanza from Goldie Hawn's memoir, A *Lotus Grows in the Mud*.

> Happiness was always important to me. Even at the young age of eleven, it was my biggest ambition. People would ask, "Goldie, what do you want to be when you grow up?"
>
> "Happy," I would reply, looking in their eyes.
>
> "No, no," they'd laugh. "That's really sweet, but I mean . . . what do you want to be? A ballerina? An actress maybe?"
>
> "I just want to be happy."[4]

The adults would invariably dismiss her reply, presuming Goldie didn't understand the question. She, however, understood the question quite well. The mentor I cited essentially intimated I didn't understand what I was experiencing. Happiness wasn't part of his equation. As I have matured professionally and personally, I've come to recognize that this mentor was not the only well-intentioned individual who didn't fully understand work and how we are meant to experience it.

Have you ever taken an employee opinion survey? Whether through formal surveys, focus groups, or informal feedback, employers regularly seek insights into employee attitudes about their jobs and their workplace. The objective is to identify areas of employee satisfaction and dissatisfaction. These surveys are also utilized to gauge *job satisfaction*. The inference is this: organizations want satisfied employees, and employees are contented with feeling satisfied with their overall work experience. Job satisfaction is a measure of employee sentiment about factors such as compensation, workload, training, resources, culture, and management. While these factors address many common concerns of employees, they invariably fail to answer the question that matters most. Are employees regularly and fully engaged in work that is meaningful?

When you hear the term *satisfied*, what comes to mind? I tend to think of an experience that is adequate or sufficient. It implies a minimum proficiency. The truth—and the challenge—is, we expect to be satisfied. Our experiences, real or perceived, often fall short of our expectations. This is particularly true when it pertains to external incentives such as compensation, benefits, or promotions. And while these external incentives can be quantified, they aren't the things we value most in the long run. Job satisfaction is too low a bar for how we spend most our waking hours. Gallup rightly asserts job satisfaction simply isn't enough to propel mission. More importantly, job satisfaction is a far cry from being fully engaged and experiencing joy in our work.

Measuring job satisfaction is akin to asking married people how satisfied they are with their spouse. Better still, it would be like devising a survey to gauge marriage satisfaction. The answers, while informative, are unlikely to provide deep insight into the health and intimacy of the marriage. Now if you ask the same individual to describe how they express their love to their spouse and how their relationship has evolved over time, you'd gain deeper insight into the health of their marriage. In marriage, love is so much more than a feeling. It similarly is an attitude of the heart. Love, like joy, expresses gratitude. This special attitude of the heart occurs when we are fully engaged in work. Real work provides meaning, peace, and wonder. That's the kind of work that deserves our time, talent, and tenacity. That's the kind of work that gives us joy.

YOUR VOCATION IS CALLING

The term *transform* is the third essential word. *Transform* means to change or convert. With respect to work, the transformation entails a change of mindset. Many factors affect our external work environment, but you are accountable for your soul at work. Many factors contribute to work productivity, but you are accountable for your required contribution. Many people and circumstances impact your work experience and the beauty revealed through your life's work. However, only one person determines your joy: you. If you want to truly experience joy in your work, you only have one person to deal with: yourself! You are the only person standing in the way of experiencing joy in your work.

Work requires effort and at times may involve difficult conditions and great challenges. We have the potential to transform our work experiences, but it will only occur if we change the way we think about ourselves and how we think about our work. *Transform* is a verb or action word. My objective is to challenge, encourage, and inspire you. Specifically, this book will challenge you to engage in deep personal introspection, encourage you to have a healthy attitude when facing inevitable challenges, and inspire you to view your work as a calling or vocation. We must identify and change things about our attitudes so that we can flourish. We must accept that we have the responsibility and the power to change them. If we truly seek joy in our work, we will find it.

This transformation also entails a conversion of personal character. Work is not simply about fulfilling duties or earning income. We have been conditioned to expect and even seek external incentives to do great work. There is, however, immense intrinsic value derived from work performed well. Work plays a vital role in character formation. The path to discovering joy in work intersects with our journey of self-discovery. Work in all its forms helps identify and cultivate interests and skills. Work also helps uncover attitudes of the heart and shape values and morals. We must deposit the best of who we are into our work each day. When we elevate our mindset and develop our character, we effectively transform an occupation into a vocation. This kind of transformation leads to greater productivity and greater fulfillment in our work.

We are all divinely created, imbued with power and purpose. When we discover purpose in our work, we find joy as well. This joyful attitude is infectious—spreading emotional, mental, and spiritual health to humankind. This type of joy is glorious, honoring God our Creator, who blesses us in and through our work.

ON MY JOURNEY

My perspective of work is informed by the full complement of my work experiences. I began working odd jobs at the age of twelve and moved on to formal part time jobs and internships beginning in high school. Post college, the nature of my employment has ranged from salaried positions to sole proprietorships principally focused in business and finance. Over the course of time, I've worked in a wide variety of environments ranging from small private firms to large public companies. A sample of my paid work experience includes the following jobs: mowing lawns, shoveling snow, washing cars, cutting hair, sorting mail, selling magazines, filing medical records, performing audits, analyzing financial statements, trading bonds, selling stocks, developing investment products, publishing books, and managing business ventures. I've experienced great joy in unassuming jobs and deep unhappiness in highly coveted roles. I have therefore come to believe all honorable work offers the potential for both professional growth and personal fulfillment.

My vocational journey continues to evolve with different assignments, changing circumstances, and new seasons of life. I would love to attest that I have arrived at my oasis of vocational bliss. That, however, is not my testimony. As with any journey, my vocational experience is marked with highs and lows. The difference at this stage of my maturation process is I know the source of true joy and how to kindle joy through my work. I have greater contentment today than at any point in my professional life. I am passionate about my work and I more readily recover from inevitable mental and emotional setbacks. I realize my work experience is part of my perfecting process. My gratitude for this instance of grace is part of the reason why I experience greater joy in my work and also my motivation for sharing my perspective and my journey.

Our character, calling, and convictions affect how we view and experience our work. On the greater path toward self-discovery, we build character, answer our callings, and live out our convictions. This is also the pathway toward discovering joy in our work. And through this perfecting process, we transform our occupations into our vocations.

May you be fully engaged in work that brings you joy.

PART ONE

YOUR WORKPLACE

The LORD God took the man and put him in the
Garden of Eden to work it and take care of it.

GENESIS 2:15

The Bible is the most extraordinary book ever written. This compilation of manuscripts, written over the course of two thousand years, has over forty known authors and countless contributors. It is, however, much more than a religious tome. From a literary standpoint, it is a work of art—the operative word being *work*. There is a divine symmetry that flows through the entire masterpiece that weaves together the principal themes and personal anecdotes. It has proven to be a source of profound wisdom, persistent truths, and practical instruction to religious and nonreligious people the world over. The apostle Paul, a prominent New Testament writer, captured it best when he wrote, "All scripture is God-breathed and is useful for teaching, rebuking, correcting and training so the servant of God may be thoroughly equipped for every good work" (2 Tim 3:16-17). It should then come as no surprise the Book reveals timeless insights about the purpose and practice of work.

The opening biblical narrative establishes work as a central theme of Scripture and a principal responsibility of humankind (Gen 1–2). The setting is somewhat chaotic. The earth is described as formless and void. It lacks any apparent sense of order and beauty. Yet the earth is teeming with endless resources and potential; there is a major task at hand. As such, we do not find God at rest, rather we find God at work. At this point of the narrative, we don't know very much about God. What is unmistakably clear to us is that God is creative and productive. Our fundamental understanding of God's nature and character are revealed to us through God's work. As the narrative unfolds, we also observe something very telling about God's attitude toward work. By every account, it can only be described as joyful. We might liken this depiction of God to that of a proud father. The created world literally springs to life as God carefully works through the intricate details of the reformation project. God's delight is apparent as he admires the work product, remarking that it is very good. God takes great pleasure in work performed well and in seeing an assignment brought to its proper completion.

The crowning achievement of God's creation process is the formation of humankind. One writer affectionately describes us as God's handiwork (Eph 2:10). God is depicted as the source and sustainer of all living things. The narrative takes great care to depict the special treatment given to humankind. Like a father figure, God forms the first human with his own hands and in his express image. The proud father deems no other work more important, and thus he gives it his undivided attention. God imbues humankind with his Spirit, equipping us to serve as careful stewards of the earth and all life forms therein. This, in fact, is the original commission to humankind. Increase in number, be productive, and rule over all other life forms. God created equal beings with complementary roles and qualities to work in partnership to carry out their commission. God also created humans to rule over other life forms but to serve humankind. This has important implications for working in community. We are designed with god-like qualities that are best reflected through our character and our work.

In keeping with the fulfillment of their purpose, the first human couple is intentionally placed in a garden in Eden. At this juncture they received their first assignment: to cultivate and protect the garden. The Garden of Eden is regularly depicted as paradise. While this characterization indeed holds truths, it is more accurate in my view to refer to the garden as the workplace of the first humans. Scripture is silent on many inferences about the Garden, but explicitly states that the Garden contained all the provisions humankind needed to be healthy and productive. The Garden also contained things that were off-limits and could even be harmful if misused. The Garden produced abundantly. But the garden required upkeep and protection. The Garden was the place where the first humans were assigned to grow and flourish. Their introduction to work was taking care of the Garden, and thus the Garden was their workplace.

What does this extraordinary ancient text have to do with discovering joy in our work? When you ask people how they feel about their work, in most instances they talk about their work environment. If you listen closely, much of the satisfaction or dissatisfaction people express about their "jobs" has less to do with the work product and more to do with the work environment. Many of the attitudes people form about their work stem from their real and perceived experiences with the people they work with and the conditions in which they work. The workplace, as most people view it, simply isn't a paradise. Well, I've got news for you. Neither was the Garden of Eden. At least not in the stylized way most people think. Most workplaces, like Eden, have what I would describe as "paradise potential." However, just as the first workers discovered, the workplace with all its potential comes down to what you make of it.

As you consider your experiences in the workplace, start with the practical realization that you will encounter challenges and triumphs every day. I defined *work* as mental or physical effort done to achieve an intended result. Neither challenge nor triumph defines work, but we certainly encounter both in our efforts to achieve our career objectives. In the poem "If—," Rudyard Kipling describes a mature individual as one who can meet with triumph and disaster and treat these two imposters the same.[1] Whether the result of relationships with coworkers, interactions with customers, changes in working conditions, or the decisions of senior management, you will meet the imposters of challenge and triumph in the workplace. Your response in these moments—and moreover, your view of the workplace—is both important for your professional development and foundational for experiencing joy in your work.

Note that I have referred to "joy in your work" as opposed to "joy at your workplace." Your work environment matters and should be chosen wisely. However, we must first examine our perspective of the workplace and not the workplace itself. One person's prison can be another person's paradise. The difference is attributable to relative perspective as opposed to relative experience. God's intent for work, workers, and the workplace is inherently good. We are meant to experience success and joy.

Our practical work experience is shaped by four factors: *attitude*, *approach*, *aptitude*, and *achievement*. In this first section of the book we will examine these four A's and the impact they have on both our views of and experiences in the workplace. Our objective is to challenge our deeply held beliefs and expectations about the workplace, seeking a fresh perspective. In doing so we will be equipped to make wise choices regarding the workplaces where we best flourish and to take better advantage of opportunities to flourish whatever the workplace. As a beloved mentor often encouraged me, we must seek to bloom wherever we are planted.

CHANGE YOUR
ATTITUDE

*Work is not man's punishment. It is his reward
and his strength and his pleasure.*

GEORGE SAND

D o you remember your first day of work? I distinctly remember the day I started my first "real" job. I was hired as a financial analyst for an investment banking firm headquartered in New York City. Though I had completed an internship with the firm the prior summer, I had a lot to learn about the business and culture. I looked forward to meeting my new coworkers and was excited to begin my career. I'd carefully read all of the literature about the company's vision and mission. I was proud to join the company and determined to make a good first impression. While I naturally had some anxiety, I don't recall any negative sentiments about work or the workplace. I couldn't wait to begin the workday.

When I arrived at the office, I made every effort to look and act my very best. My business unit focused on trading securities such as stocks and bonds, so I dutifully read the market sections of the leading daily newspapers. This wasn't about career ambition or office politics. (Selfish motivations would reveal themselves soon enough.) My mindset on the first day was naive, but my motivation was pure. I was grateful for the opportunity to engage in meaningful work. Though it was fleeting, I experienced joy in the workplace.

Was your first day similar? Do you recall similar emotions and thoughts about work and the workplace? Now let me ask you a different question. Reflect on your last day at work, or any recent day for that matter. Is your joy waning or gone? Let me pose the question a different way. As you prepared for work, were you eager to get to the office—or just late? Were you looking forward to spending time with your colleagues? All of them? When was the last time you reviewed the vision statement of your employer or reflected on the mission with pride? Do you actively seek opportunities to encourage or mentor others, or are you primarily engaged in office gossip and politics? Do you feel grateful for the opportunities and resources provided by your employer, and how—if at all—do you express your gratitude?

If your current answers differ from your first day responses, I offer two pieces of advice: Don't be discouraged. And please keep reading. The practical reality is that each day in the workplace can't and won't be like the first day. However, each of us has the power to make all our days in the workplace productive and fulfilling.

IT'S ALL ABOUT ATTITUDE

What accounts for the difference between that first day at work and your more recent days? I have heard people offer many answers to this question. In times past, I've offered many answers myself. The first and most common refrain ascribes our initial perspective to naiveté. In other words, our current emotions, thoughts, and actions reflect reality—specifically, the sometimes-harsh realities of the workplace. Isn't that why people dream about retirement? The second common refrain is that things in our workplace have changed. Invariably, we have a negative or adverse reaction to the changes. From our viewpoint, things are not as good as they used to be, and thus we are less satisfied or even dissatisfied. The final refrain is often some version of "woe is me." Whether through promotion, compensation, or choice assignments, I don't perceive that my contributions have been adequately rewarded. My career plan is not turning out how I'd envisioned, and it adversely impacts my views about the workplace. While these are all plausible responses, they ultimately fall short in a very important dimension. None of them address the first step on the road to joy in work, which is being content in the workplace.

It is certainly the case that our coworkers and work environment differ from what we initially perceive and even hope about them. This dissonance between what we expect and what unfolds isn't inherently good or bad, although we tend to place value judgments on outcomes that differ from our expectations. We fail to realize it is often our own unrealistic expectations that adversely impact our view of the workplace. It is also true that our workplaces and, more specifically, the cultures of our organizations are constantly changing. While the pace may vary, organizations evolve over time. Ignoring or resisting change is counterproductive. It is far better to anticipate, embrace, and wherever possible impact the changes of your organization. A proactive approach to change has profound positive effects on our workplace experience.

Finally, it is a safe bet your career plan will not unfold the way you've envisioned. You can look no further than your own résumé as proof. Career accomplishments unquestionably bring you temporal happiness. Unfortunately, they don't provide long-term satisfaction and they don't give you joy. We all would do well to distinguish career accomplishment from career fulfillment. It turns out each of our common refrains, though true in part, lead to discontentment if unchallenged.

So what accounts for the difference between that first day in the workplace and your most recent day? Recall the four factors that shape our work experience: *attitude, approach, aptitude,* and *achievement. Attitude,* the first of the four, accounts for all the difference. While the people and the company are constantly evolving, in most instances they haven't changed dramatically. Granting some exceptions, an organizational mission likely hasn't changed significantly since we joined the enterprise. The things we observed on our first day and every day after have most likely evolved in modest, predictable ways. As far as change, the only thing that undoubtedly has changed is our attitude.

By *attitude* I am referring to the way we think about our work and our workplace. With little time spent on reflection, we often fail to perceive the changes in our own disposition. We imperceptibly change our view of our coworkers, career opportunities, and even the mission of the organization. Our experience in the workplace is shaped by how we choose to see it. In many respects, it is our attitude that makes all the difference.

ATTITUDE ADJUSTMENT

"Teachers Quit Jobs at the Highest Rate on Record." This *Wall Street Journal* article recently caught my attention.[1] The article reported public educators voluntarily leaving their jobs at the highest rate in nearly two decades. Concerns over pay, poor working conditions, and increased opportunities given the tight labor market were cited as drivers for the trend. I hold educators in high regard given the important role they have played in my vocational journey.

I decided to contact Lisa, a long-time friend who teaches elementary school in Florida. Lisa is one of the most cheerful people I know. She has a gift of discernment and her optimism is contagious. I asked her, "Why did you become a teacher?"

Lisa quickly replied, "I never gave serious thought to becoming a teacher until I was in college. I was walking through a room with shelves filled with books and for a moment I was completely transfixed. I heard a quiet voice from within say 'You are supposed to be a teacher.' The next day I went to my advisor and changed my major."

Lisa explained that she believed teaching was her calling. As an educator, she doesn't simply instruct. She believes she is called to love, serve, and inspire her students. Lisa acknowledged that teachers face some formidable challenges. In her case, she finds it difficult to deal with the bureaucracy that is common in public education. I asked, "What causes you to continue given the challenges?"

"I focus on the students. The most rewarding part of teaching is when one of my students accomplishes something he once felt was impossible. This attitude shift can create a ripple effect of success in his life." Her response is apropos to the consideration of our workplace experience. Her disposition not only impacts the attitudes and achievements of her students, it leads to an abiding sense of calling and fulfillment in her work.

Lisa's example raises an essential question. Does your workplace need to change, or can you change the way you see it? I am not suggesting your experience in the workplace will always be peaches and cream. Far from it. We each bring our strengths, weaknesses, passions, and problems to the workplace daily. Each of our proverbial houses has rooms that need improvement and those developmental opportunities are generally more evident to others than to us. As the Scripture goes, we see in a mirror, dimly (1 Cor 13:12). Some might ask, What happened to paradise in the workplace? *People* happened to paradise in the workplace. However, if you view it through the right lens, you realize that the essential link between humanity and the workplace is a good thing. It's one of life's most precious gifts. The opportunity to unite with a shared vision and engage in meaningful work is uniquely human. Yet the common enterprise is not without challenges. The workplace, not surprisingly, reveals our humanness in all its facets. However, the potential of the enterprise is infinitely greater than the individual. How we choose to see the workplace establishes our foundation for working in community and discovering joy in our work. We must learn to develop the proper attitude toward the workplace.

Let's focus more intently on our attitude. *Attitude* refers to our mindset or manner of thinking. It is the first of four factors that shape our experience in the workplace. As the first of the four factors, it is foundational. We will explore three attributes of attitude to better understand how it impacts our experience in the workplace. First, attitude is an inherent quality of our minds. Attitude emanates from the inside and is a portrait of one's inner self. Second, our attitude determines our perception. Specifically, it determines how we view other people, our circumstances, and ourselves. Like the way an optical lens affects our physical eyesight, attitude affects the perception of the mind's eye. Third, attitude influences our emotions, behavior, and decisions. In fact, our emotional welfare, conduct, and choices on any given day are principally a reflection of our attitude.

Because our attitude is an innate quality, our experience in the workplace has more to do with our disposition than what happens to us on any given Monday. Attitude is not merely about wishful thinking, and there is no one-size-fits-all approach for developing a healthy attitude. Developing a healthy attitude is, however, an essential component of experiencing fulfillment in the workplace.

IT'S AN INSIDE JOB

The first attribute of our attitude is that it emanates from the inside and is nurtured by our inner self or thought life. I have come to the stark realization regarding my attitude and the workplace that many of my perceived bad days in the workplace begin before I ever arrive at the office. Similarly, many of my most fulfilling days also begin before my commute to the office. The instigator in either case—as you may have guessed—is my attitude.

Let me share an example. I returned from a business trip after enduring two extended flight delays. I missed what I'd hoped would be quality time with my family, who were all fast asleep when I arrived home. After getting just four hours of sleep, a scan of my calendar revealed my first meeting of the day was with Jack, a colleague who has a working style I personally find challenging. As I prepared for work, my mind was busy choreographing a play that ran several times in my head before I boarded my commuter train. I concluded Jack was not particularly collaborative and thus our pending meeting would be an unproductive use of time. In fact, we simply have too little productivity in the company, I surmised. How do you think that day turned out? You probably have a good sense of how my workday unfolded without knowing a solitary detail because you've identified the real culprit: my attitude!

That day did not produce my best work. The meeting with Jack was predictably challenging. Did Jack's approach contribute to the challenging interaction? Quite possibly. However, my view of the meeting was somewhat predetermined. What's more, it may be the case Jack had a very different view of the same meeting, work styles notwithstanding.

I've also noticed there is a bit of a momentum factor as it pertains to our attitude in the workplace. It's sort of like Newton's first law of motion. Once an object is in motion, it continues in motion at the same speed and same direction unless acted on by an outside force. When we begin the day with a negative attitude or disposition, it tends to chart the course for that day. This is in large part because our attitude is driving us from the inside. We are less affected by the events occurring around us than we believe. It turned out my engagement in other meetings that day was notably subdued and the number of nagging items in my inbox seemed to multiply exponentially.

By highlighting the essential role our attitude plays in our workplace experience, I do not seek to diminish the very real challenges regularly encountered in the workplace. Interpersonal conflicts, discrimination, and harassment are common and potentially systemic challenges individuals face in the workplace. These types of situations often require mediation and corrective action. In fact,

if you find yourself in the midst of a toxic or abusive situation in
the workplace, seek counsel and intervention immediately. Yet
even in the midst of situations that cause real pain, the right attitude equips us to respond in proactive and constructive ways.
The understanding that our attitude emanates from the inside is
very empowering. It means we can start each workday with positive momentum if we so choose. If we set our day in motion with
a healthy attitude, it's likely to stay on track. It also means when
we encounter injustice or related problems that require addressing,
an intentional disposition will frame and guide our response.

Newton's law of motion has one more helpful insight I believe
can be applied to our attitude—the concept of the unbalanced
force. An unbalanced force is synonymous with a greater force. An
equal and opposite force will bring an object to a standstill.
However, an unbalanced force can change the momentum and
direction of an object. This suggests if we start our day with a
negative disposition, it takes an outsized effort to turn it around.
To be clear, you *can* turn a bad day around. Don't throw in the
towel if you get off to a rough start. However, it is wise to observe
this: a healthy attitude provides positive momentum that is relatively easy to maintain during the day. This has clear implications
for how we approach our physical health. I believe, however, there
are even greater implications for how we approach our mental and
spiritual health, understanding they are all inextricably connected.

Starting the day with a healthy attitude toward work is not
about positive thinking per se. Instead, it is about having an affir-
mative plan for tackling the triumph and challenge to be expected
with each day. It is also trusting that whatever the new day brings,
the opportunity to do meaningful work is an instance of grace.

TAKE A CLOSER LOOK

Our attitude determines our perception of people and circumstances. Throughout each day, we are constantly interpreting the

actions, words, and even facial expressions of the people we interact with. This begins from the time we are born and is an essential aspect of human interaction. We also must discern how to respond to the dynamic circumstances that unfold daily. How we respond to people and how we react to ever-changing circumstances depends on how we perceive or view them. Moreover, this interpretive work is principally happening at the subconscious level of our mind. If attitude is the filter for the mind's eye, we must accept that our attitude may at times deceive us. At the very least, we must be aware that our attitude may mislead us. By that, I mean all we see is not always all there is. Additionally, our preconceptions and biases can lead to misperception.

The quality of our interactions and ultimately our relationships with the people we work with arguably has the greatest impact on our experience in the workplace. If you don't believe this straight away, consider how a single interaction or even an offhand comment from a coworker affects you mentally or emotionally. We are, after all, human and by our very nature highly relational. Our attitude impacts our relationships with others in a two-fold manner. It is the filter by which we interpret their actions and words. It also depicts the image we project to others. Our attitude often introduces us or precedes us.

How we perceive our work environment also has a significant impact on our experience in the workplace. To maintain the proper motivation and remain productive we must perceive we are in a healthy work environment. It is impossible to find joy in our work if we do not have a constructive view of our coworkers and our work environment. Since we spend many of our waking hours at our workplace or on activities related to work, this has carryover implications for our quality of life.

A particular experience from several years ago sheds light on how my attitude affected my relationship with a coworker. My business unit head asked me to update our executive team on an important initiative I was leading. The project involved working with professionals across multiple business units in the company, and most of them were not in my reporting line. I articulated our progress to date, which included some notable successes and milestones, as well as some identified challenges. In the middle of the overview, my colleague John chimed in with an unexpected and curt critique. I honestly felt blindsided because John had not directly been involved with the initiative and hadn't previously shared his perspective with me. As I listened to John, I could feel myself tensing up. What was his motivation for what I perceived as an ill-informed assessment? Why surprise me in front of my manager and peers when he had ample opportunities to speak to me beforehand? Even though I did my best to provide a balanced response, my response was defensive. While the exchange was short, the effect lingered with me for the rest of the workday. That evening my wife asked me why I seemed somber during dinner. It was then the change in my attitude was most apparent.

Later during the week, I decided to speak with John about his perspective on the initiative. I made sure to prepare myself mentally to remain open-minded. I've found attempts to presume the motives of others are wasted mental energy. It is far better to have candid and direct engagement. I learned several things from our dialogue. The first thing I learned was there were opportunities for me to involve John in the initiative I hadn't previously considered. This would not only gain his support but provide him with a firsthand perspective. John acknowledged in retrospect his comments were precipitous. He was newer to the team and felt pressure to contribute to the dialogue. I hadn't considered the pressures John was under as a new member of the team. John apologized for his brusqueness without me specifically raising the issue. This was a surprising turn of events. We can never fully know what is in the heart of another individual. In many ways, it doesn't matter. We must simply do the work of examining our own heart and our own attitude. Maintaining an open mind and a positive disposition helps us better understand the people and situations we encounter. This is an important contributor to maintaining good relationships and a positive workplace experience.

IN THE BACKGROUND

Our attitude influences our emotions, behaviors, and decisions. Our parents are often the first to impart this pearl of wisdom to us. Whether when I was throwing a tantrum as a child, being naughty as an adolescent, or acting obnoxious as a teenager, I can remember a common refrain from my parents: "You need to change your attitude!" Depending on the nature of the infraction, the statement was more demonstrative. Interestingly, while they observed erratic emotions, uncharacteristic behavior, or poor decisions, they intuitively addressed the root of the issue, which was my attitude. Though we make several thousand decisions in a typical day, most of them are automatic. Even when we put our cognitive skills to work and thoughtfully consider our choices, our attitude is influencing us in the background. This is similarly the case as it pertains to emotions and behaviors. Our attitude predisposes certain emotions and certain behaviors. I am much more likely to become angry or respond abruptly to a coworker if I begin the day with a negative attitude. I'd like to tell you those early pearls of wisdom from my parents made for smooth sailing in adulthood. As it turns out, I had a lot to learn about this thing called attitude. In fact, I'm still learning.

Have you ever been a recipient of an email reproof? That's when you open your inbox and discover an accusatory email from a coworker. It usually involves an implicit or explicit expression of blame. There may not necessarily be actual proof of an infraction. But in the internet age, people often hit send and ask questions later. Sandy was a senior research analyst with my former employer who collaborated with our sales team on a client initiative. Sandy determined a significant client relationship was at risk because we had fallen behind schedule on the project. Sandy's email—directed to me—highlighted an apparent missed deliverable by a member of my sales team as a notable failure. To add injury to the accusation, a host of individuals were copied on the email, including several members of upper management. It's interesting to observe how such a passive form of communication can get the adrenaline flowing. I was a new sales manager and felt a strong sense of accountability for the actions and welfare of my team members. I perceived Sandy's action as more political than constructive. Finally, I was concerned about the reputation of the accused and our overall team. I responded by email immediately using "reply all." (This is never a good idea.) In retrospect, it was one of the worst communications I've ever sent. All the points I made were accurate. But my communication was verbose and defensive. It was an emotional retort rather than a thoughtful response.

There is a proverb that admonishes us not to answer people according to their folly, lest we become like them (Prov 26:4). This was unquestionably true as it applied to my situation. Sending the accusatory email was imprudent, especially so given the accusation was unfounded. It was equally imprudent for me to respond so hastily. It didn't help matters that I also copied the group. I suspect I am not the only person who has made this mistake. This experience initially taught me a lesson about restraint. Over time it has revealed deeper truths about attitude. When we maintain a healthy attitude and properly manage our egos, we are not easily offended. We can't control the behavior of others, but we are accountable for our own actions. Our emotional and behavioral responses are most effectively managed when we adopt and maintain a positive attitude toward our coworkers. This is a function of personal development that must take place long before the inevitable surprises and challenges that arise. Just like when we were children, we need to "change our attitude" to ensure emotional stability, constructive behavior, and wise choices.

BEING CONTENT

In the search to discover joy in work, a healthy attitude toward our coworkers, workplace, and our work itself makes a huge difference. Work is not a burden but a blessing. It builds strength of character and gives us pleasure that cannot be found in leisure activity.

I conclude with one final lesson about our attitude in the workplace, also imparted by a wise woman. Early in my career I was promoted to a prominent role with a leading investment banking firm. My work revolved around the financial markets, and it was customary for my days to start before daybreak. The first individuals I met daily when I arrived in the office were our security staff. In fact, the lobby of the building was often empty save those dedicated professionals. There was one woman who made a significant impression on me. Debra was an older African American woman who was distinguished by her warm, broad smile. I don't recall a single day where she didn't project a joyful attitude. Unlike her fellow security officers, she would kindly greet everyone as they arrived. Whether you responded cordially, smugly, or not at all, she'd always wish you a blessed day. One morning, shortly after the September 11 terrorist attacks, I arrived at the office in a somber mood. There was Debra to greet me, just as pleasant as the first day I encountered her.

I'm not sure what prompted it, but I felt compelled to ask Debra about the source of her apparent joy. I came right out and asked her, "Debra, you're always so joyful. Most of the people I see are gloomy early in the morning, especially after the recent terrorist attacks. But you never seem to have a bad day. What's your secret?"

She pondered my comment for a moment and then replied. "I'm blessed to be able to work and I am thankful for this job. I've had many jobs over the years. All of the jobs have challenges. I just don't dwell on them. As I have matured, I've learned to be content whatever my circumstances."

I recognized the scriptural reference (Phil 4:11) and saw her faith helped shape her attitude. Therein lied Debra's secret to fulfillment in the workplace: contentment! To be content means we are pleased with our situation and do not feel as though we need it to be better. In our constant quest for more, we often miss the simple pleasure experiencing the present day provides. I reflect from time to time on my conversation with Debra. Her simple wisdom and living example taught me so much. Our best days in the workplace occur when we learn to be content with our circumstances. Adopting this attitude toward the workplace is an important first step to discovering joy in your work.

CHAPTER 1 REFLECTIONS

Change Your Attitude

———

KEY INSIGHTS

- True joy is an attitude of the heart that informs your way of thinking and feeling. Your perception of the workplace informs your overall work experience.

- Unrealistic expectations adversely impact your view of the workplace. Contentment leads to discovering joy in work.

- Attitude emanates from the inside and is a portrait of your inner self. Transformation begins with examining your perspective of the workplace and not the workplace itself.

- Attitude determines your perception—how you view your circumstances, other people, and yourself. Presumptions and biases lead to misperceptions.

- Attitude influences your emotions, behavior, and decisions. A healthy attitude and properly managed ego ward off offenses.

- A constructive attitude generates momentum that propels you through your workday mentally, emotionally, and spiritually.

- Work is not a burden but a blessing. It builds strength of character and gives you pleasure that cannot be found in leisure activity.

2

ALTER YOUR
APPROACH

*I put my heart and my soul into my work and
have lost my mind in the process.*

VINCENT VAN GOGH

Have you ever had a case of the workplace blues? Maybe you feel that way right now. Maybe that's why you're reading this book. Let me assure you, you're not alone. I personally experienced what I would describe as a "dry season" in the workplace. It came on the heels of a big promotion. I regularly exceeded my performance expectations and maintained a good reputation and positive profile within the organization. I received positive reviews from management and was reasonably well compensated. Outwardly, everything appeared great. But inwardly, I was in a real funk. By the end of the week I would feel mentally and emotionally drained. Increasingly, I was physically fatigued. Since I naturally have high energy and have been equally blessed with good health, this was more than a departure from the norm. This was a warning sign. The shift in my internal condition had occurred gradually, practically without notice. But the mental, emotional, and physical toll was now more apparent. I realized it was time for some serious introspection.

As I began to ponder the root cause of my despondency, all signs pointed to the workplace. The scope and breadth of my management responsibilities required a high level of employee engagement and an endless expenditure of emotional energy. I was responsible for overseeing a fast-growing business in a resource-constrained environment. My workdays had become a virtual sprint from beginning to end. Business travel, a constant throughout my career, increased in frequency and duration. This resulted in more time away from home as well as the office. On my days in the office, I regularly spent five or more hours in meetings. There seemed to be a direct correlation between the amount of time spent in meetings and the increase in office politics. Increasingly I was embroiled in interpersonal conflicts with peers or called on to mediate disagreements between my direct reports. Taken together, these circumstances compressed the time available for working toward near-term deadlines. This also left precious little time for strategic thinking. With planning reduced to a minimum, emphasis was often deferred from important priorities to urgent matters. There was clearly something wrong with the company. Or was there?

It is not uncommon to experience rough patches over the course of a career. During these seasons, you may question your fit within or value to the organization. This is true even if you are passionate about your work. A stretch assignment, a strained relationship with a supervisor, a negative performance evaluation, a relocation, and countless other circumstances can precipitate a despondent mindset toward the workplace. While this does not represent a career crisis, it is an important internal alarm that signals something is amiss. The inability or unwillingness to fight through our despondency has adverse professional and personal implications.

One of my favorite poems is "Invictus" by William Ernest Henley, which has resilience as its theme.[1] The very term *invictus* is derived from a Latin word that means "unconquered." The poem ends with the author's affirmation, "I am the master of my fate and the captain of my soul." When we encounter trying times in the workplace, we must do the intimate work of managing ourselves and the empowering work of taking accountability for our circumstances.

IT'S TIME TO MAKE A CHANGE

Something didn't fit with the bad company narrative. While my responsibilities had increased, my role hadn't fundamentally changed. My workday still involved the core aspects of what motivated and inspired me. I decided to explore that train of thought to better unpack my feelings toward the workplace. I asked myself a basic question: When did I feel most engaged at work? The first thing I identified was my outcome-orientation. It is vitally important to me to be engaged in meaningful work that produces measurable outcomes. I genuinely feel energized when I am highly productive and make progress toward clear goals. Even if the task at hand is difficult, I find the experience rewarding. Furthermore, I like problem solving and relish challenges. Working on effective teams equally energizes me. From my vantage point, an effective team commits to a shared mission and works collaboratively to ensure success. I am not particularly conflict averse and will engage candidly and transparently for the sake of realizing a shared vision. Finally, I am a natural strategic thinker, and I excel at ideation. It is important to me to be empowered, and I feel valued when I have a degree of autonomy. I was encouraged as I realized that these essential aspects of engagement were still part of my work experience.

Naturally, I asked myself the opposite question. When did I feel least engaged? The first answer was easy and could be summed up in one word, *meetings*! A significant part of my workday was spent in meetings. Since most of our work required collaboration, meetings were necessary and valuable. However, if a meeting does not have a clear purpose and move toward a clear decision or action, it can prove unproductive or even counterproductive. The frequency and perceived effectiveness of the internal meetings were mentally fatiguing. The second thing I observed was I often felt emotionally drained on days that required a high degree of interpersonal engagement. There were certain days when I was figuratively out of gas. Initially, I was perplexed as I am an extrovert and, on the surface, a natural people person. Upon closer introspection, I am actually a moderately expressed extrovert with a rational temperament type. For example, I am intellectually curious with a deep love for reading. As such, I need quiet time to explore ideas as well as to emotionally recharge. Finally, I was least engaged when I did not feel empowered in my areas of responsibility. This is not surprising given how much I value accountability.

As I reflected on my engagement in the workplace, the heart of the issue came into focus. My time, talent, and tenacity weren't being applied toward their highest and best uses. I felt as if I had less influence over my daily routine and fewer decision rights. I was faced with some adversity with respect to managing my workload and navigating political issues within the organization. There wasn't anything wrong with the company per se. My old plan wasn't adequate for my new circumstances, and thus my true challenge was managing myself. This is not to say I lacked discipline. I was working harder than ever and applying proven disciplines that had served me well throughout my career. That was the rub, so to speak. The workplace is dynamic. As our role, responsibilities, and circumstances change, we must adapt accordingly. I decided I didn't want or need a new position. But it was clear I would have to make some changes.

In addition to having a healthy attitude, we must employ effective practices to attain fulfillment in the workplace. The second of the four A's, your *approach*, holds the key to adapting to new challenges. By *approach*, I mean the way you manage your responsibilities and your relationships in the workplace. Organizations generally evolve in measured, predictable ways. However, your unique situation may change significantly or unexpectedly. Maybe you've been given a new assignment that requires new competencies or skills. Maybe you've been reassigned to a new department and you must develop relationships with new clients and coworkers. Maybe your company is undergoing a reduction in force and you are feeling the pressure of rising expectations and resource constraints. Work goes beyond our job description or performance expectations. It extends to the mental effort required to develop the proper approach for a given set of circumstances. Good things happen when we combine the right attitude with the right approach.

The famous Dutch artist Vincent van Gogh spoke profoundly when he said, "I put my heart and soul into my work and lost my mind in the process."[2] His words resonate with my personal experience. Do they ring true for you as well? Van Gogh was a prodigious painter credited with 2,100 artworks, most of which were completed in the last two years of his life. He neglected his physical health and suffered from mental illness. Though he became extraordinarily famous posthumously, he only sold one painting during his lifetime. There have been times when I have felt as though I'd given my whole heart to my work and lost my way in the process. At times I've failed to constructively manage the demands of the workplace, leading to emotional distress. I've had enough conversations at the water cooler to know I'm not alone. Developing the wherewithal to alter my approach has contributed significantly to improving my workplace experience. I have discovered I must alter the way I *prepare*, *prioritize*, and *partner* to turn distress into success. We will explore these three aspects of our approach to our work to gain practical insight into improving our overall experience in the workplace.

PROPER PREPARATION

How well prepared are you for each day at work? It seems like a simple enough question. It was frankly something I took for granted early in my career. Yet upon careful review, I realized I wasn't nearly as prepared as I thought. Proper *preparation* requires intentional effort to ensure the proper mental approach. Some of us by temperament are natural planners and others are not. I admittedly am wired as the planning sort. Whether you are a natural planner or more planning averse, a little proactive preparation can go a long way. The required preparation varies depending on the task or objective. For example, if I am working on a marketing campaign for a product launch, I must prepare mentally to engage in a creative process. Preparation for leading a management meeting may entail identifying clear objectives beforehand. Measurable objectives establish mental guideposts to focus the team's efforts. Preparation often entails identifying action steps that lead to mutually beneficial outcomes. While most of us have a clear sense of what we want to accomplish, we often fail to consider the perspectives of everyone involved. Identifying a win-win approach that benefits multiple stakeholders can serve as the catalyst for moving an important initiative forward. In each of these instances, the quality of the preparation is a principal determinant of the quality of the outcome. Better preparation leads to better days.

A variety of factors contribute to the quality of our preparation. One might ask, what's the key to proper preparation? In my own work experience I've settled on one essential principle: start with the end in mind. This is the key to proper preparation. In my line of work, I frequently deliver presentations and speeches. I begin my preparation by clearly defining the target audience and establishing the core message. What impact do I want to have on the listener? This is the specific end I envision in mind. This informs my deliberate process of preparation. My preparation includes researching the subject matter and drafting a detailed outline.

Following this, writing ensues. Significant time is devoted to preparation. The mental picture of the audience impact drives the preparation and ultimate delivery. This principle applies to any form of work we engage in. Starting with the end in mind ensures proper preparation and ultimately leads to purposeful performance.

PUTTING THINGS IN ORDER

I'd like you to tap into your power of imagination for just a minute and envision your next day at work. As you look forward to that day, what will you need to accomplish? What are the goals or objectives for that day? What tasks do you need to complete for you to consider that day a success? What expectations do your coworkers have of you and what dependencies do they have on your work? What urgent requests or unexpected events might you encounter? You can get fatigued just thinking about the volume of demands each day. You may have noticed another subtle truth about your experience at work: work, it turns out, is more than just showing up. If your workplace is like mine, ever-changing demands greet you each day. Given that your time is a limited and relatively fixed resource, your effectiveness is a function of how you spend it. This reveals another important facet of our approach to work. *Prioritization* is vitally important for your success and fulfillment in the workplace. Prioritization is essential because it allows us to prudently allocate our most precious resource: our time.

Prioritization involves determining the order of dealing with things according to their relative importance. Prioritization is both prudent and pragmatic. It is prudent because we demonstrate wisdom by identifying the objectives and actions that will contribute the most value to our common mission in the workplace. Some things truly are more important to tend to than others. Prioritization is pragmatic or rational because of one of our most basic human tendencies. We are overly optimistic. While optimism is a valuable mindset, we regularly overestimate the number of tasks we can complete in any given day. This means we invariably end the day with some things left undone. This raises a critical question. What is left undone? If we do not tend to the essential task of effective prioritization, our efforts in the workplace are less effective and less fulfilling. Let's face it. One of the simple pleasures in our workday is checking an item off our to-do list. It is all the better when we prioritize and can draw emotional energy from completing objectives most valuable to the organization.

Stephen Covey is credited with illuminating a profound principle which he demonstrates visually with big rocks and little pebbles.[3] When you tend to the priorities or big rocks first, it creates more space for tending to the lesser priorities or the little pebbles. One of the most useful habits I have adopted is scheduling blocks of uninterrupted time during the workweek for proactively contacting clients, which is essential for our long-term business success. Regularly attending to prioritization is not simply prudent or pragmatic. It can have profound effects on our experience in the workplace.

DON'T WORK ALONE

The third and final aspect of our approach to work is from my perspective the most essential. I'd like you to tap into your imagination once again. I'd like you to call to mind several of your most fulfilling experiences outside of the workplace. Think of times when you've felt you were part of something very special, when you had a strong sense of accomplishment, when you were happy or triumphant. Better still, think of times when you were overjoyed. I want you to hold those recollections for a moment and similarly recall your most fulfilling experiences in the workplace. Think of times when you felt your contributions were appreciated and recognized, when you contributed to a noteworthy accomplishment or successful initiative. Think of times when you weren't merely satisfied but you experienced joy in the workplace.

Why are these experiences so memorable? What attributes of these experiences make them so fulfilling? How might these experiences shape your approach to future opportunities?

When I consider my own recollections outside of the workplace, I have lasting memories of events such as successfully representing my elementary school on the debate and academic bowl teams. I recall several unforgettable athletic experiences when teammates rallied for hard-fought victories. I recall the immense joy I felt at my undergraduate and graduate school commencement ceremonies. And I recall my first book project, which I co-developed with a dear friend. When I consider some of my more fulfilling career experiences, I have many to choose from. I recall early in my career working on a financing that was instrumental in saving a company from bankruptcy and changed the fortunes of the business going forward. I have fond recollections of working with a group of coworkers to revitalize a nonprofit our company supported. And I have a fond recollection of celebrating the listing of a new investment fund our team launched on the New York Stock Exchange. These and countless other experiences have not only been fulfilling, but they speak to my deeper purpose for engaging in meaningful work.

What do my experiences have in common? None of them would have been possible without the power of *partnership*. To *partner* means to work jointly on an activity or initiative. It means to combine forces becoming a greater force. Partnering is not simply being cooperative but actively seeking allies and welcoming assistance. No single personal or professional experience of consequence I can point to would have been possible without partners. Whether the teachers and tutors who helped me to succeed academically or my teammates in extracurricular activities, we were allies in our pursuit of common goals. When successfully launching new products or initiatives in the workplace, I've worked collaboratively with teams of talented people. And even at times when I've struggled or fallen short of workplace expectations, there have been coworkers or mentors there to offer words of encouragement and lend a helping hand. Partnering, it turns out, is fundamental to being successful in the workplace and it is essential to finding fulfillment personally and professionally. People, as I like to say, are designed to work in partnership.

What does all this talk about partnering have to do with how we approach our work? I've found in times of stress, we can unwittingly draw inward when we need to reach out. Managing a challenging situation or discovering an innovative solution is easily within my reach if I am willing to reach out to others. I recognize that temperaments differ, but partnering is not a function of extroversion or introversion. Different personality types partner in different ways. As partnering goes, opposites indeed often are attracted to productive ends. Effective partnering may involve delegating, collaborating, aligning, or simply asking for assistance. Partnering may be achieved in group settings or one-on-one. Whatever the tactic, the key is to understand you don't have to go it alone. Partnering is not simply a means to an end. It is so much more. It turns out valuable work and memorable experiences are not only made possible through partnership, they are made meaningful through partnership. When we demonstrate the willingness and ability to practice partnering, we change the very fabric of the relationships we have with others in the workplace. Building alliances unleashes the greatest power available to you, the power of the human spirit.

HOW HAPPINESS HAPPENS?

"I just tendered my resignation to Brent," said Mark. "I value our relationship and wanted you to hear this directly from me." Though employee turnover is commonplace, Mark's departure was an utter surprise. I had recently been named as head of the business unit. Mark, who managed one of our top-performing investment groups, was identified as a rising star. Brent was Mark's supervisor and a member of our management team. Just the prior week, he'd advocated to further expand Mark's responsibilities. I composed myself and turned my attention to this urgent matter. "Mark, you are a highly esteemed member of our team. Will you please help me understand the reason behind this decision?" "I have been treated well with respect to promotions and pay. And before anybody asks . . . it's not about Brent. The job has just really worn me down. Frankly, I haven't been happy here for a long time."

Mark had all of the markers and trappings of success. Yet when the covers of his psyche were pulled back, it revealed a discontented attitude toward his work and workplace. How did this occur? We spent the next hour unpacking his views. Mark, a natural introvert, spent much of his career as a research analyst and portfolio manager. Over a period of five short years he received several promotions and took on general management responsibilities. He had grown frustrated with the pace of change at the company and felt misaligned with certain aspects of the culture. While he still relished the intellectual rigor of his work, he'd soured on the managerial and relationship management aspects of his position. Ironically, it was Mark's unbridled career ambition that led to his increased management responsibilities. Each promotion, however, resulted in a shift away from the aspects of his vocation he most enjoyed.

Over the next several days, we worked diligently to retain Mark. But he had signed a letter of intent with his new employer, and our efforts were ultimately unsuccessful. I appreciated his many contributions and wanted to maintain our relationship. I met with Mark on his final day to wish him well and offer perspective for his continued career journey. "Mark, I want to thank you for your service, and I wish you continued success. I do however encourage you to reflect on your stated desire to find greater fulfillment in your work. For me, fulfillment is largely a product of my attitude and approach toward my work." I am reasonably confident that Mark will do well in his new role. He is exceptionally talented and very driven. The jury is out as to whether Mark will find greater meaning in his work and contentment in his new workplace. The verdict will have less to do with his choice of employer and more to do with his approach.

Mark's story is not exceptional. The employee life-cycle often looks something like this: Jane Doe is hired by an employer of choice. She is quickly promoted into a coveted new position. Jane's manager and coworkers assume things are going very well. Unexpectedly, Jane resigns and divulges she has been unhappy the entire time. There are plenty of legitimate reasons why we may feel unhappy in our workplace. However, if we feel our work or our workplace is making us unhappy, we must take initiative. In many instances, the most useful actions involve changing our approach. Again, our approach entails how we manage our responsibilities and our relationships in the workplace. Altering your approach to preparation, prioritization and partnering improves the nature and quality of your work. Changing your approach also enables you to develop your skills while growing personally and professionally. And if you subsequently decide to change your employer or oc-cupation, you are more likely to remain on the path toward dis-covering joy in work.

CHAPTER 2 REFLECTIONS

Alter Your Approach

———

KEY INSIGHTS

- Trying times in the workplace demand the intimate work of managing your emotions and the empowering work of taking accountability for your circumstances.

- Work includes the mental effort required to develop the proper approach.

- Good things happen when you combine the right attitude with the right approach.

- Proactive preparation goes a long way. Better preparation leads to better workdays.

- Prioritization allocates your most precious resource: time.

- Partnering with others allows you to combine forces, becoming a greater force.

- Partnering involves actively seeking allies and welcoming assistance from others.

3

RAISE YOUR APTITUDE

Whatever your life's work is, do it well.
A man should do his job so well that the living,
the dead, and the unborn could do it no better.

Martin Luther King, Jr.

Employers across the globe know the workplace is people-powered. A shared mission is foundational. Desirable products or services are required. A clear strategy is vitally important. However, corporate success is ultimately determined by the attitudes and actions of the employees. Engaged employees take positive actions to further the mission of the organization. Employee engagement is not only key to propelling the enterprise forward, it is also vital to experiencing joy in work. Much of the research regarding employee engagement is an outgrowth of a broader discipline or science known as "talent management." This discipline addresses how organizations attract, develop, and retain talented employees with the express objective of achieving current and future goals. There is an important word recurring in this narrative, the term *talent*. Employers certainly want and need employees to be engaged. But they are not simply seeking to attract, develop, and retain any type of employee. They are seeking talented employees who will become highly engaged in the shared mission of the organization. It turns out matching talent with need is harder than it might seem.

What are employers seeking when they search for talent, and what talents do employees offer to enrich the workplace? As a hiring manager, I focus on expertise, leadership potential, and interpersonal skills when assessing talent. I begin by assessing demonstrated expertise in the functional hiring area such as marketing or finance. I try to ensure candidates are both knowledgeable and intellectually curious as this will ensure their acumen will grow over time. Leadership in large part involves the ability to effect positive influence, and an individual can demonstrate leadership in any position. Given this outsized impact, I place a premium on leadership potential. Finally, I assess interpersonal skills. We require good relationships and a healthy community to do our best work. This is why I focus on qualities such as humility and a proven track record of effective teamwork. From my perspective, these aspects work together as markers for talent.

While the term *talent* can be defined in a variety of ways, it is synonymous with *aptitude* in this context. *Aptitude* refers to our human capacity to learn or to do something. It reflects our competence in an activity or occupation. Aptitude reflects our innate abilities as well as our acquired skills. At times, we contribute our natural gifts and inherent genius to the workplace. We similarly contribute our acquired expertise and qualifications. Aptitude, cultivated through personal and professional development, is the most valuable resource in the workplace. Just as organizations only thrive if they successfully attract, develop, and retain talented people, increased aptitude expands an individual's career opportunities, enhances professional achievements, and leads to greater fulfillment in the workplace.

SHORT SUPPLY

"[Global] talent shortages continue unabated," remarked Jonas Prising, chief executive officer of ManpowerGroup.[1] This observation was part of an introduction to the company's 2015 Talent Shortage Survey. ManpowerGroup is a professional services firm that provides human resource solutions for companies around the world. Their areas of expertise include recruitment, training, career development, outsourcing, and workforce consulting. The company slogan is "powering the world of work." The nature of the firm's mission, along with its global network, provide a unique perspective for assessing issues impacting the workplace. The firm offers custom solutions for recruiting and retaining talented professionals. An area of emphasis is the recruitment of professionals who possess skills in high demand. This expertise informs the firm's research around talent management. As I explored the concept of aptitude and its relationship with joy in the workplace, their annual survey on talent shortage caught my attention. Previously, we considered the prospect of a global engagement crisis in the workplace. Is there an impending talent crisis as well? Is talent increasingly in short supply?

For the past decade, ManpowerGroup has studied global talent shortages and their impact on the workplace. The tenth annual edition surveyed nearly 42,000 hiring managers from forty-two countries and territories around the globe. About 38 percent of the hiring managers cited having difficulty filling positions, a number that has been rising for the past seven years. One of the most consistent themes over the ten-year history is that certain categories present acute challenges. Roles that perennially have been hard to fill include skilled trade workers, sales representatives, engineers, technicians, executives, and drivers. Aside from the impact of some structural economic forces such as low unemployment rates or demographic shifts, the biggest cited reason for difficulty filling these needed positions is a lack of technical competencies. This

mismatch of need and skill has notable impacts on hiring companies, including lower productivity, reduced competitiveness,
and a diminished capacity to serve the needs of customers. As I
became familiar with the survey results, a truth came into view. If
we define talent as a specific set of qualifications related to a dis-
cretely defined role, then the talent organizations seek is indeed
limited. If we define talent more practically as aptitude, then a
significant opportunity exists for prospective employers and employees. In many respects, the valuable research by Manpower-
Group reveals an incredible opportunity to match organizational
aims with individual aptitude. The research suggests investments
in training and development by both prospective employees and
employers can help to close the real and perceived talent gap. It
also underscores the third of four factors that shape our experience
in the workplace. Aptitude matters.

Although I did not participate in the survey, I am an experienced hiring manager. I have had the privilege of hiring talented
individuals at companies where I have worked and as a proprietor
of my own business. Like many hiring managers, I have developed
meticulous job descriptions that specified required competencies
and experience. This was generally followed by painstaking
searches for candidates with just the right qualifications. As it
turns out, I have rarely hired the hypothetical candidate described
in the job specification. To be clear, I have hired some exceptionally talented individuals. These individuals have possessed the
core competencies required for the varied positions although their
résumés haven't exactly mirrored the job specifications. While I
can't say every hiring decision has resulted in a good match, most
have worked out very well. Those results are not principally because of my prowess as a hiring manager, although I'd like to believe I contributed favorably. The reason these hires have worked
out so well is that people come with talents that can't be
dreamed up in a job specification. Their innate abilities and

acquired competencies are often greater than we or they realize. Moreover, their aptitude is not a fixed commodity.

I had the privilege of hiring a finance officer who increased the effectiveness of our leadership team in ways we could not anticipate. Everyone knew Zara was great with numbers. What was not fully appreciated was Zara had a keen strategic intellect and was adept at navigating teams through complex decisions. Zara enabled our management team to better identify growth opportunities and make the tough decisions to retrench from legacy businesses. She also helped revamp our hiring practices. The power of people is most exemplified by their potential to exceed even the highest expectations. Zara is a senior executive in the company today and continues to exceed high expectations.

A SWEEPING SUCCESS

Martin Luther King Jr. is an iconic historical figure because of his transformative leadership in the civil rights movement. While he is principally remembered as a champion for social justice, his vision was more expansive. Economic justice and empowerment were areas of principal focus, albeit efforts cut short by his untimely death. While Dr. King fought for equal opportunity in the workplace, he also preached individual responsibility. Specifically, he charged people of every creed, ethnicity, and social class to seek economic empowerment. He believed we each have a moral obligation to serve humanity through our occupation. He believed we should always endeavor to do exceptional work.

On October 26, 1967, just months before his assassination, Dr. King gave a speech to a group of students at Barratt Junior High School in Philadelphia, Pennsylvania. The theme of the speech was "the blueprint for life." He provided inspiration and wise counsel as these youths considered future personal and professional pursuits. Dr. King shared this now-famous anecdote, which he offered on more than one occasion.

If it falls to your lot to be a street sweeper, sweep streets like Michelangelo painted pictures, sweep streets like Beethoven composed music. . . . Sweep streets like Shakespeare wrote poetry. Sweep streets so well that all the host of heaven and earth will have to pause and say: Here lived a great street sweeper who swept his job well.[2]

Dr. King admonished those young people to pursue nothing short of excellence in their work. The metaphor of the street sweeper is powerful because it underscores his belief in the dignity and value in every type of work. While effort is important, his admonishment wasn't simply an appeal to work hard. His words were a charge to fully commit their hands, heads, and hearts to their work. His charge echoes today and is relevant for each of us. Though using different words, I believe Dr. King also embraced the essential importance of aptitude. Our aptitude, which combines natural ability with acquired competencies, is more than a means to earning a living. Aptitude enables us to excel in our work. When you discover, develop, and deploy your aptitude, others will take notice. The unique value only you can offer is both a gift to you and to those served through your work. Through the perfecting and providing of your gift, you experience joy. Therefore aptitude is a key factor in experiencing joy in the workplace.

THREE PART HARMONY

Let me offer you some aptitude encouragement. You are more talented than you realize. No matter where you are in your life's journey or what you've accomplished to this point, you have a deep well of talent from which to draw. You have creative potential yet untapped. You have endowed gifts yet uncovered. You can learn new competencies through instruction. You have interests that have not been fully explored and purpose yet to be revealed. So how do you raise your aptitude? Aptitude represents your capacity to learn or do something. This is the basis for my three-part framework of *discovery*, *development*, and *deployment*. I refer to this simple, yet effective approach as "the 3D method." You must discover, develop, and deploy your talent and then repeat the process in order to thrive in the workplace. Discovery requires self-awareness. You discover your talent through purposeful introspection. Development requires discipline. You hone your talent through coaching and training. Deployment requires effort. You intentionally utilize your talent to create value and to serve others.

My father was a supervisor in the workplace and has served as a pastor for many years. His responsibilities often involve counseling, mentoring, or teaching others. He taught me that the surest way to master a concept was to teach it to someone else. He views opportunities to teach and mentor others as valuable opportunities to increase one's aptitude. He also believes if you have been blessed with the capacity to acquire knowledge and practical wisdom, you have a communal responsibility to share with others. In our household, we were taught to pay it backward and forward with respect to our possessions, money, and talent. Beginning with my parents, I have been the beneficiary of prudent instruction from wise mentors. Their example and instruction have played an essential role in enabling me to continually increase my aptitude. As my father foresaw, some of my most valuable lessons have come as a result of mentoring others. Not only have I experienced the intangible rewards that come from helping others grow, I have further increased my own aptitude in the process. Considering this, I will share several real-life examples of the 3D method in practice to encourage and assist you as you seek to increase your own aptitude.

DISCOVERY CHANNEL

About eleven years ago, I met a very bright young woman who'd just been hired by our company. Catherine was a little over a year removed from her undergraduate studies, having completed a short stint with another company. She was enthusiastic and intellectually curious. She had a natural optimism that shone through on any interaction. She was outgoing and adept at relationship building and networking. In fact, Catherine leveraged her personal network to land the opportunity with our company and we first connected through her networking efforts within the company. Over the years we remained connected, and I observed her career progression. Like most millennials, Catherine craved variety and new challenges, assuming diverse responsibilities over the course of her tenure. She was viewed as a high performer and received several promotions. She also developed a good reputation among her coworkers and had strong sponsorship from several senior managers.

There was just one small problem. She was uncertain about the direction of her career. After nine years and several positions, she didn't have a clear sense of where she wanted to go with her career. There were also changes in her personal life she had to consider as she pondered her next career move. Catherine shared her concerns with me and asked me if I would mentor her. We agreed to a formal mentoring engagement over the course of the following year, provided she was open to a nontraditional approach.

I began our mentoring engagement by simply listening. Catherine outlined three things she wanted to accomplish. The first was to better align her interests and talents with her roles and responsibilities. The second was to become a more effective communicator in the workplace. The third was to articulate some principles to guide her career choices. After identifying her goals, I shared my approach toward my career advancement and the philosophy I took toward mentoring others. I suggested the clarity she sought concerning her career path was most likely found through thoughtful introspection. I used this as an opportunity to introduce the first stage of the 3D method, discovery. She agreed to independently take several assessments that I suggested would inform our discussions and move her down the path of self-discovery. We began with a temperament assessment tool that provides insight into how an individual communicates and works in teams. Our temperament is the part of our character that affects our predisposition or state of mind. It is most regularly reflected in observable traits such as habits, communication styles, and interests. The Myers-Briggs Type Indicator is historically a widely recognized indicator while my preferred offerings are the Keirsey Assessments.[3] Given her transparency and natural curiosity, she quickly embraced and employed suggested tools and counsel regarding self-discovery. She noted that in prior mentoring engagements she generally asked questions and received instructions or advice as to what she should do. During our interactions, I served more as a guide. I provided useful methods, asked thoughtful questions, and offered unique perspectives.

Over the length of our engagement, I witnessed Catherine grow professionally and personally. While she maintained her winsome attitude, she was more focused and intentional. At the onset of our engagement, she was anxious about her career path and presumed she needed to move out of the internal consulting function she was working in. By the end of yearlong engagement, Catherine had not only determined she was well placed but was promoted to expanded responsibilities within the group. To be sure, the credit goes to Catherine for her intentional effort. She not only developed in her functional area of consulting but more generally demonstrated greater clarity and confidence in her communication. She even divulged that many of the concepts we discussed she applied at home with her family.

I also benefitted from mentoring Catherine. First, it reinforced my conviction regarding the purposeful process of discovering talents. People all too often look outside for answers that only can be found within. Raising aptitude depends on our purposeful and continuous search to mine the reservoir of talent that has been deposited in us. The great news is there are people and tools to help us along the way. Second, it was an important reminder of our need to remain open and curious. If you want to raise your aptitude, you must be open to fresh perspectives and new approaches. Finally, I was able to personally grow through supporting another person's development. Working with Catherine through the process of self-discovery presented valuable opportunities to reflect on my personal journey, which is a work in progress. Gaining a deeper understanding of oneself is the principal objective of the discovery phase of the 3D method.

DEVELOPMENT OPPORTUNITIES

Entrepreneurship provided me with developmental opportunities that differed from my experiences in the corporate sector. One such opportunity related to talent management. During my tenures at large financial services companies, I've had the benefit of entire departments of professionals dedicated to assisting me in the recruitment and retention of talent. When I owned a small business, I saw the human resources department each time I looked in the mirror!

One of our very first hires was a sales associate who worked for our retail business. Lewis was connected through a familial relationship and was striving to make ends meet with a part-time job. When I interviewed Lewis, he was engaging and possessed a natural charisma. He was also kindhearted and had a service orientation. Having been in sales for much of my early career, I pegged him as a natural salesperson. Lewis became one of our first hires. It turned out he was indeed naturally inclined toward sales and service. We soon discovered he was creative and had a diverse set of talents. He was well-liked by customers and coworkers. But while he displayed a great attitude and a multitude of talents, Lewis lacked discipline.

When I refer to a lack of discipline, it wasn't acts of commission. Lewis was very respectful, and truly had a heart for service. He nevertheless regularly made omissions through inadequate attention to details. I took a vested interest in his development because it was plain to see he had a lot of potential. Though we didn't initially consider it a formal mentoring arrangement, we began to spend time outside of work hours engaging around personal and professional development. The operative word is *development*. I used this as an opportunity to introduce the second stage of the 3D method. As I learned more of his personal narrative, I realized Lewis hadn't received much in the way of formal training. He had plenty of raw talent but lacked the tools and coaching necessary to cultivate his abilities.

Lewis had recently completed a class offered by his church on discovering areas of giftedness. I suggested he take the StrengthsFinder assessment developed by researchers at Gallup as a complement.[4] The StrengthsFinder assessment is designed to uncover natural talents or strengths that can readily be translated to competencies valued in the workplace. With the results in hand, we pursued an intentional plan for increasing his aptitude in his areas of strength. We also worked on disciplines to improve his ability to focus and his attention to detail. Lewis could not have been a more willing student. He was also very gracious in that my method was hardly refined. We each made up in effort what we lacked in experiential knowledge. It was truly development at work.

Lewis worked with us for nearly four years before he moved on to a better career opportunity. We were blessed to have him and could not have been more pleased to contribute to his professional development. We went on to design a training program for our store employees built around some of the 3D concepts, with a focus on development. My business partner, who was gifted in program implementation, put formal tools in place to support our associates in increasing their aptitude.

Although we are many years removed, I keep close tabs on Lewis. He has experienced various changes in his career and has a wonderful family with four children. I learned several important lessons from our time together. The first and by far most important thing I learned is the importance of being teachable. His example far outweighed many of the eloquent things I've read or heard on raising your aptitude. Second, I learned the vital importance of receiving honest and actionable feedback. Lewis was ready and willing to grow professionally and personally. He just needed candid feedback, genuine encouragement, and a little guidance. We each must be willing to openly seek feedback and thoughtfully provide feedback so our workplaces flourish. Finally, it reinforced the necessity of personal discipline. I can't attest that practice makes you perfect. I can, however, attest that practice will perfect you. Personal discipline is essential for the development phase of the 3D method.

DON'T DELAY DEPLOYMENT

As a corporate executive, I've had the opportunity to manage several businesses. Hiring and developing young professionals is a critical element of long-term success. Rubin was an aspiring young professional hired as an investment analyst for a growing business I managed. Intellectual and with a reserved demeanor, Rubin was proficient in his core responsibilities, which involved the analysis of investment funds and the marketing of those products. His manager noted that Rubin regularly produced high quality work. Despite these traits, the feedback about Rubin was mixed. While he was regarded as smart and reliable, his level of engagement was questioned. He was also perceived to have a dispassionate attitude and communication style. During a luncheon meeting with several of our young associates, he voiced several career concerns.

After consulting with his manager, I decided to engage with him more intentionally. Rubin readily acknowledged his effort and attitude were inconsistent. He knew he had more to offer, but he felt stifled in his current role. He didn't believe his contributions were fully appreciated. He cited this as the reason for his uneven engagement. He was also eager to be promoted to the next level of seniority within the company.

I offered Rubin some constructive and candid feedback regarding his performance as well as how he was perceived. I observed he wasn't fully deploying his talents. One example was that Rubin was a connector and had a large network of associates across the firm. He could easily leverage his contacts and resources to help his team members but rarely availed himself. Rubin was also a good technical writer, and we were in short supply of that skillset as we sought to increase the number of our investment publications. This was another area where he could make immediate contributions. Rubin's reluctance to fully *deploy* his skills limited his professional development and adversely affected his overall work experience. I offered him a vital piece of advice I received early in my career: provide a level of service that exceeds your level of pay. This is the path to promotion. I assured him if he was fully committed, I would personally coach him.

We began by taking inventory of his aptitudes, dividing them into three groups, and examining the core competencies required for his role. Next, we discussed which of his acquired skills were underutilized. Finally, we considered which of his natural abilities could be better deployed to enhance his contributions. I suggested Rubin complete the Kolbe A™ Index Assessment, which evaluates an individual's instinct-driven behavior or natural way of doing things.[5] The objective was to help him better deploy his talent in the workplace. We also targeted opportunities to deploy his leadership capacity among the associates in the group. My general approach was to guide him by asking questions and offering perspective.

As Rubin began to earnestly deploy his diverse talents, I observed several notable changes. The most notable change was his more positive disposition. Rubin felt his contributions were valued, and it showed. He was invited to contribute in new and different ways. His colleagues were complimentary of his attitude and aptitude. Deploying his talents helped him become more intentional regarding his professional development. Over the course of two years, Rubin acquired two professional designations and completed a second master's degree. Along the way, he received the promotion he desired. More significantly, he was offered a new role with substantially more responsibility and pay.

When I consider his journey, Rubin made tremendous strides in a short period of time. What was particularly rewarding about our engagement was the personal impact it had on him. He didn't simply become more proficient. He found greater purpose in his work. I daresay Rubin experienced joy in the workplace. Helping him along the path gave me joy as well. To be clear, I'm no Pollyanna. Intentionality with respect to deploying your skills may not directly lead to increased pay or promotion in the short run. I do, however, believe you can derive tangible and intangible long-term benefits if you borrow from Rubin's example.

First, you must be personally accountable. It's easy to see yourself as a victim of unfair or unfortunate circumstances. However, you have both the power and the responsibility to increase your aptitude. An individual may determine your level of pay or the timing of your promotion in the short run. However, you are the only person who determines the degree to which you learn and grow professionally.

Second, raising your aptitude requires self-awareness. You must commit time to getting to know yourself. You must also realize you cannot fully achieve this alone. We all need the support of colleagues and mentors to help us fill in our blind spots in order to progress.

Finally, increasing your aptitude is not optional. It is an implicit expectation in the workplace. Increasing your aptitude requires effort. You owe that effort to the mission and the people you serve. Most of all you owe that effort to yourself. Deployment increases your aptitude by putting your talent to productive use. When you put your talent to work, it works for you.

I've had the benefit of learning from exceptional mentors. I've also enjoyed the privilege of mentoring remarkable individuals. The breadth of these experiences suggest talent is abundant if you know where and how to look. Our self-knowledge is incomplete, however, and we have the opportunity to become enlightened. This applies to our disposition, behavior, and talents. To increase our aptitude, we must discover our talents. Once our talents are revealed, they must be developed and deployed. Deploying our talents has less to do with the nature of our work but rather the quality of our work.

In his powerful speech on the blueprint for life, Dr. King espoused the integration of work and life. Whether our life's work is to sweep streets, design the buildings that tower above them, or negotiate business transactions from the suites overlooking them, he gave us the same charge. "Do it so well that the living, the dead, and the unborn couldn't do it any better."[6] This is what fully deploying your talents entails. It is a sure method of increasing your aptitude and a sure path to discovering joy in your work.

Raise Your Aptitude

KEY INSIGHTS

- Engage with talented people who commit to do great work and provide exceptional service.

- Your aptitude, which is a function of your natural abilities and acquired competencies, is the unique skillset that enables you to excel at your work.

- Your aptitude is a gift to you and to those around you. Use your gift.

- Aptitude is cultivated through personal and professional development. To thrive in the workplace, you must discover, develop, and deploy your talent.

- Discovery requires self-awareness. It entails a purposeful search to mine the reservoir of talent that has been deposited in you.

- Development requires discipline. Commit to providing a level of service that exceeds your level of pay. This ensures personal growth and often leads to promotion.

- Deployment entails putting your talent to productive use and reflects the quality of your work.

4

ENSURE YOUR
ACHIEVEMENT

*There is joy in work. There is no happiness except in the
realization that we have accomplished something.*

Henry Ford

W asting Time at Work: The Epidemic Continues."[1] This was
the title of an online article that piqued my interest, given
the subject matter and my exploration of joy in work. The article
asserted that employees wasting time at work is a deepening problem
for employers. The lost productivity resulting from disengaged or
distracted employees was described as a workplace epidemic. The
article referenced two surveys, one sponsored by CareerBuilder and
the other by Salary.com. These surveys provided perspectives from
both employers and employees on how time is spent in the workplace. Both surveys indicated that employees spend substantial
time on non-work-related activities during the workday. This
likely comes as no surprise if you are among the legions of people
who show up to the workplace daily. As such, the premise of the
article is not particularly controversial.

One underlying finding is, however, very instructive. Employees
are quite busy during their time in the workplace. They, while
admittedly not always productively engaged in their work, are

active nonetheless. This suggests the real issue is less about a wide-spread aversion to perspiration and more a lack of true inspiration. People are yearning for meaningful work. Let's explore what the surveys say.

SURVEYS SAY

The CareerBuilder survey included 2,200 hiring and human resource managers and just over 3,000 workers ages eighteen and over.[2] Participation was limited to full-time US workers from the private sector. The survey revealed the top ten contributors to wasted time in the workplace and the implications of the lower productivity. The most telling finding was that three of four employers estimated two or more hours a day of lost productivity due to distracted employees. Among the top distractions were texting, social media, internet browsing, emails, meetings, and good old-fashioned gossip. The wasted time turns out to be costly, with employers citing negative consequences including compromised work quality; negative client and employee relationships; and lost revenue. While the reported findings were chiefly presented from the employer perspective, the responses from the workers surveyed corroborated the general findings regarding workplace distractions.

Salary.com conducted the second survey cited.[3] The company's survey for "Why & How Your Employees Are Wasting Time at Work" complemented the CareerBuilder survey, given the responses were exclusively from the employee perspective. Of the 750 workers surveyed, 89 percent admitted to wasting some time at work. I am, however, intrigued that 11 percent of respondents purportedly don't waste a single minute at work. The most striking finding was nearly 6 in 10 workers admitted to wasting one or more hours daily. How did they waste time you might ask? The same way most people do. The top reported productivity inhibitors were social media, internet browsing, unproductive meetings, water cooler conversations, and returning emails. The

CareerBuilder and Salary.com surveys were consistent on two basic findings. Workers are increasingly distracted, and the types of distractions are quite common.

The survey results present a few dilemmas for employers. For starters, managers often surmise results differ among demographics. I've heard many strong opinions from managers on this topic. Managers have asserted younger professionals are more readily distracted and female employees are more apt to socialize at work. This is where empirical findings are handy. The survey results suggest age matters little as it pertains to distractions in the workplace. The seasoned fifty-year-old employee was just as likely to waste time as the spry twenty-year-old employee. Single employees spent slightly more time on non-work-related activities, but the differences were not material. What about gender? Statistically there was little difference in the findings for women and men. For the record, men reported wasting slightly more time than women in the workplace. How did employers respond to the growing distractions and adverse impact on productivity? The most common responses were to restrict the use of company resources and implement stricter rules of conduct. Employers blocked internet sites, monitored emails, banned personal calls, and narrowly scheduled breaks. The challenge with such authoritative responses is they are generally interpreted as disempowering to employees. This ironically contributes to disengagement, which in turn makes employees more susceptible to distractions at work.

WHY ASK WHY?

It occurred to me that much of the analysis emphasized who, what, when, where, and how. However, the most valuable insights arguably resulted from one basic question: Why? Why do employees waste time at work? The workers surveyed generally offered one of four reasons for seeking distractions at work. The most common reason was feeling burned out. Many workers feel physically, mentally, and emotionally strained by the demands placed on them. Couple this with office politics, bureaucracy, and resource constraints, and it is understandable that over 50 percent of the employees cited this as the primary reason they seek distractions. While employers view this as wasted time, employees often perceive it as cause for acceptable breaks. The second reason workers seek distractions is simply boredom. About one in five individuals surveyed did not find their work challenging or interesting. The third reason individuals sought distractions at work was because they felt as though there was no incentive to work harder. This applied to monetary and nonmonetary incentives alike. In short, they didn't feel effort was appropriately acknowledged and rewarded. The fourth reason workers seek distractions is they are unsatisfied with their jobs. A respected mentor described these as instances when employees "quit and stay." Their discontentment with their role leads to distraction and disengagement.

A cynic could surmise many people simply don't want to fully apply themselves in the workplace. I do not, however, accept the slacker theory. If we thoughtfully consider the perspectives of the workers surveyed, we uncover a different narrative. Individuals yearn for meaningful work. Their motivations extend beyond simply earning a living. If workers devote most of their waking hours to the workplace, it should come as little surprise they want that investment to truly count. It is important to note employees are equally frustrated by low productivity in the workplace. Albeit they have some differing views from their employers as to the root causes as well as the methods for improving. Employers can underappreciate that workers have a vested interest in improving productivity. In fact, the survey findings suggest workers are seeking a greater sense of achievement. They want a clear correlation between their efforts and the output of the enterprise. They want to know those efforts are acknowledged and valued. They want their employers to remove unnecessary obstacles and distractions that impact their ability to focus on their work. Finally, they want to experience the simple joy that comes from a job well done. Why are workers increasingly distracted and even disengaged? Just maybe they're seeking more joy in their work.

A WINNING TEAM

Henry Ford, founder of the Ford Motor Company, is remembered as one of the world's foremost industrialists and for his revolutionary approach to assembly line production of the automobile.[4] Though Ford invented neither the automobile nor the assembly line technique, his reinvention of work processes and culture enabled the mass production of affordable automobiles. He was a visionary credited with business innovations such as the franchise system, which put dealerships throughout the United States as well as six continents around the globe. While Ford championed the mass production of cars and other goods to make them more affordable, it was his overall approach to the employee experience that accounted for his enduring impact on the workplace.

One example was his approach to incentives. He believed in high wages for workers. As his business matured, he offered pay twice as high as the typical daily wage. Ford also was among the first to introduce a reduced and standardized workweek. Ford first shifted to 8-hour workdays then to a 5-day workweek and is credited as a primary force in establishing the common practice of the 40-hour workweek. His motives were not purely altruistic. Ford believed providing more leisure time for employees was good for business in two important ways. The increased leisure would promote better physical and mental welfare, improving productivity. Furthermore, the workers who were seeing unprecedented growth in their income would also be more likely to purchase the company's products. Ford's genius in many respects was less about automobiles and more about productivity in the workplace.

Continuous and necessary improvements in productivity cannot be achieved simply through implementing technological advances or altering business processes. Today's workplace is ultimately people-powered. Henry Ford seemed to instinctively understand that essential truth. He married his revolutionary production techniques with equally revolutionary approaches for incentivizing and motivating his workforce. While he utilized external incentives such as attractive wages and increased leisure time, he also recognized the importance of intrinsic motivation. He recognized that people are inwardly motivated to strive for achievement. He knew from his personal experience that achievement had to be tied to work the individual found fulfilling. He saw this as an intrinsic motivation for those he hired. Toward the later stage of his successful career, he focused on management philosophy and the employee experience. He believed employees should thrive in the workplace. True to his values, he viewed productivity and achievement as essential contributors to one's success and joy in the workplace.

Recall the four factors that shape our experience in the workplace. *Achievement*, the fourth and final factor, enables productivity and is the cornerstone of personal fulfillment in the workplace. Our achievements are the results produced by our efforts. In the introduction, we defined *work* as mental and physical effort applied to achieve an intended result. Achievement is properly framed in the context of attaining an envisioned outcome. *Achievement* is not synonymous with *activity*. Activity without progress may indeed qualify as a distraction but doesn't quite qualify as productive work.

The surveys previously cited disclosed a variety of unproductive activities that occur in the workplace. When we successfully finish a task, reach a goal, or complete a mission, we know we have accomplished something worthwhile. We have the inward knowledge that both our effort and our output are good.

Measuring achievement is the way we keep score in the workplace. That winning feeling we associate with achievement is more valuable than remuneration or recognition. It is a measure of joy we find in our work. Henry Ford—wittingly or unwittingly —tapped into a remarkable truth. Our work offers us a different kind of joy than our play when we collaborate with others to achieve a shared goal.

RUNNING FOR JOY

I have always embraced hard work. I like to say I am wired for work. I have a strong achievement orientation that drives my personal and professional pursuits. A dear friend once observed that my preferred leisure activities seem more like work. How you interpret that remark depends on your view of work. His remark was insightful in this respect: you learn a lot about an individual based on how they spend their time. About twelve years ago, I stumbled onto what has become one of my favorite pastimes. Our family had moved to the friendly confines of a quiet suburb. We were surrounded by forest preserves and bike trails that provided ample opportunities for outside activity. Eager to shed a few unwanted pounds around my midsection and improve my fitness level, I decided to add running to my routine.

My first run was physically and mentally challenging. It was naturally difficult because I was not in running condition. I was thoroughly winded by the time I reached the first mile marker. However, there was something else at play. I didn't have a clear goal and felt as if I was running aimlessly. I realized I had to generate some internal motivation or else my running days were numbered. That very evening, I signed up for a local 5K race. My goal over the next month was simple. I would run three days per week with the objective of becoming fit enough to complete the 5K run without stopping. I didn't set a time objective for my first race. The goal was simply to finish.

With that simple goal in hand, I completed the race and received a small medal. I was so proud of that little medal. I signed
up for several more races that summer, ending with a 5-mile race.
Over the next several years, I progressed from 5-mile courses to
10-mile courses and then to running half marathons. Over time I
entered fewer official races, opting for the serenity of running
alone. This time with nature provides wonderful opportunities for
reflection and meditation. I relish the physical challenge as well
as the spiritual rejuvenation. I wouldn't have predicted I'd become
an avid runner. I realize this pastime aligns with my natural
achievement orientation. As with many runners, I eventually set
my sights on completing a marathon. Completing my first Chicago
marathon still ranks as one of my most memorable personal
achievements. I've completed a total of three marathons and numerous other long-distance races.

While each experience has been unique, three common lessons
are essential to completing the course. First, you must plan to
finish. Second, you must run your own race. Third and finally, you
must keep your mind on the prize. I have come to accept these
lessons as essential, also, for achieving meaningful goals in the
workplace. Let's study all three lessons as we advance to the finish.

CROSSING THE FINISH LINE

The first lesson I learned is this: you must plan to finish. Completing a marathon does not require an exceptional level of athletic ability. It is true, some individuals are naturally inclined
toward distance running. It is also true that some people have
physical barriers or limits that prevent distance running. Nonetheless, many average Janes or Joes have the potential to complete
the course. Whether you're a natural athlete or a couch potato,
you must employ the right plan to make it to the finish. My marathon plan involved eighteen weeks of training. The schedule
required measured increases in mileage with the peak coming

several weeks before race day. While many people highlight the required long runs, the discipline of following the plan is the key to achieving the goal. This includes committing to a healthy diet and healthy sleeping habits.

How does this apply to achievement in the workplace? You must plan to be successful. It takes discipline to achieve clearly identified goals. Many individuals expect their talent to drive results. However, talent alone isn't enough. The discipline applied to preparation and performance daily leads to achieving desired outcomes. This discipline extends to our personal lives as well. Committing to a healthy lifestyle is a key contributor to ensuring we are at our best as we pursue our vocation. Our personal and professional disciplines are the key to achieving important goals.

The second lesson I learned is you must run your own race. When I toed the line for my first marathon, nearly forty thousand participants joined me. There is naturally a fair amount of anxiety and excitement as you set out to achieve something you've been preparing for diligently. When the race begins, it is easy to fall into running the pace of contestants most proximate to you. One of the keys to persevering is running the race for which you've trained and sticking to your game plan.

Achievement in the workplace is similar. We all have defined roles and responsibilities. We also have areas or conditions in which we thrive. Work environments can be stressful or competitive at times. It is easy to allow anxiety or insecurity to creep in. This may cause us to behave in a manner inconsistent with our values or cause us to drift from our defined role or responsibility. Achieving shared goals and outcomes in the workplace requires us to fully commit to our assigned role and responsibility. It also requires us to be true to our values and to trust our coworkers to be true to theirs. If we each dedicate ourselves to serving the mission by running our assigned race, we can achieve great things through our work.

The third and final lesson I learned is you must keep your mind on the prize. If you faithfully complete the training, you are physically equipped to complete the course. This is not to say it is not physically demanding. Your body will go as far as your mind takes you. The interesting part about running the marathon for the first time is you don't run the full distance during training. Most training plans top out around twenty miles. This means on race day you literally run further than you've ever run in a single session. Finishing requires focus and faith. When you get to the final stages of the race, the physical toll mounts. This may be further complicated by unanticipated occurrences such as unfavorable weather. The truth is, you prepared for this and you have everything it takes to finish if you don't quit. The key is focusing on the prize from start to finish.

Our experiences in the workplace are similar. Our education and training provide us with the competencies required to complete our assigned tasks. Our discipline and values enable us to faithfully fulfill our distinct roles and responsibilities. But our mental focus enables us to commit ourselves to the achievement of important work objectives.

When I think of mental fortitude in a professional context, my neighbor Ronald immediately comes to mind. Ron is an orthopedic surgeon. Orthopedics, Ron explained, is a medical specialty that focuses on the prevention, diagnosis, and treatment of injuries and disorders of the bones, joints, ligaments, tendons, and muscles. As avid runners appreciate, it is not uncommon to suffer various injuries as one adds on the mileage. It has been very fortuitous for me to have an orthopedic surgeon as a neighbor and friend. Ron has provided me with invaluable medical advice over the years and some impromptu treatment at acute times of need. Ron aspired to be a doctor from an early age. "I always wanted to be a doctor, but I really didn't have an idea of what kind of doctor," Ron explained. During his time in medical school he had the opportunity to work with many types of doctors and ultimately chose to focus on orthopedics. "I felt that the orthopedic surgeons worked hard and really enjoyed what they did," Ron observed. Driven by early visions of becoming a physician, he was no stranger to hard work. As a surgeon, Ron is often able to help patients who are injured or impaired return to high levels of function.

What impresses me about Ron's vocational journey is the discipline and determination necessary to achieve his position. His specialty required nearly a decade of higher education and specialized training before he was fully qualified to perform surgeries. I can personally attest that Ron is especially well suited for his vocation. Each insightful diagnosis and successful surgery reaffirms his calling. Crossing the marathon finish line is one of the most exhilarating feelings I've experienced. In the same manner, taking important assignments across the finish line in a work setting gives us a deep sense of accomplishment and fulfillment. This is analogous to Ron's achievements on his vocational journey. The path to discovering joy in your work is lined with the mile markers of achievement. Crossing the finish line is pure joy.

Ensure Your Achievement

KEY INSIGHTS

- Don't be distracted from meaningful work. Limit internet browsing, social media, emails, and meetings; avoid workplace gossip.

- Achievement enables productivity, leading to personal fulfillment in the workplace.

- Work offers more joy when collaborating with others to achieve a shared goal.

- Plan to finish, run your race, and keep your mind on the prize in order to accomplish your goals.

- Preparation coupled with daily discipline leads to high performance and desired outcomes.

- Shared goals and outcomes require full commitment to your assigned roles and responsibilities.

- Training provides competencies required to fulfill your role. Values enable you to faithfully carry out your responsibilities.

PART TWO

YOUR
WORK ETHIC

Satisfaction lies in the effort and not in the attainment.

Mohandas Gandhi

Once upon a time there lived a wealthy landowner who owned a large vineyard among his vast properties (Mt 20:1-16). Many of the employment opportunities in an agrarian society involved the cultivation of the land, which made the landowner a major local employer. The nature of his business created seasonal and temporary employment opportunities. One morning the employer went out in search of day laborers to work in his vineyard. After agreeing to pay the equivalent of a full day's wage, the employer sent the group to work in the vineyard. About noon the same day, the employer encountered a group of able-bodied individuals standing idle in the town square. They explained they were unable to find work for the day. The employer hired all those willing to work, directing them to join the first group presently working in the vineyard. There was no predetermined wage. The landowner simply promised to pay them an appropriate amount at the end of the workday. During the mid-afternoon and early evening hours, the employer encountered others standing idle.

In each instance, he offered them the opportunity to engage in productive work, promising to pay them a proper wage for their labor.

At the end of the day, the workers were paid in order from the last to the first hired. The first group of workers voiced displeasure with their employer because each laborer received a full day's wage. This group did not protest the working conditions or their treatment by management. They did not object to the level of pay offered. After all, they agreed to the amount upfront. They expected a higher wage because they worked longer hours. Their employer countered that he had indeed honored his promise, having paid them a full day's wage. He then posed an interesting question: Are you envious because I am generous? This response is curious to some and confounding to others. The decision to compensate all the laborers equally despite different lengths of service seems patently unfair. This assumes that the only value derived from work is monetary compensation.

While there is a deeper spiritual focus of this parable, the story also conveys a truth about the value of work. The vineyard owner understood the enduring value derived from gainful employment. When he encountered capable individuals seeking work, he offered them employment opportunities. While he was generous with his money, the true value provided was the actual work experience. The opportunity to engage in meaningful work encourages and imbues a work ethic, which is our focus in the second section of the book.

Work ethic is the principle that work is intrinsically virtuous and builds character. Specifically, the work ethic promotes qualities such as humility, dependability, and accountability. A strong work ethic espouses the moral benefit of work for its own sake and not for personal gain or reward. Likewise, we do not work merely to produce goods or provide services. Satisfaction is indeed derived from our efforts along with our accomplishments. Our deepest fulfillment is often derived through professional and personal maturity. Beyond earning a living, we work to develop competencies and character. The latter is reflected in our work ethic. In the first section of the book, we examined the four factors that shape our experience in the workplace—attitude, approach, aptitude, and achievement. My objective was to challenge beliefs about the workplace with the intent of establishing a fresh perspective. In this section, I will challenge you to examine your inner self through the prism of your work ethic. My intent is to provide an understanding of the symbiotic relationship between character formation and vocation.

How does your work ethic relate to your character and values? It all comes down to motivation. Three primary external motivations fuel our desire to work. I will refer to these as the three rewards —*remuneration*, *recognition*, and *respect*. The first reward is *remuneration*, which is simply money paid for service or work. The second reward is *recognition*. People have an intrinsic need for affirmation and are influenced by the opinions of others. The third reward is *respect*, which is a feeling of admiration for someone based on his or her qualities, abilities, or achievements. There is nothing inherently wrong with these rewards if they are appropriately balanced by a healthy set of personal values. The problem arises when our external motivations outweigh our internal motivations. Recall the parable of the vineyard workers. The first hires simply focused on their remuneration and disregarded the generosity of the vineyard owner. They didn't fully appreciate the opportunity they were afforded to strengthen their character through their work.

Your work ethic is a window into your soul. It reveals your true character and motives. Your work ethic reflects the person you have chosen to be and the person you are in the process of becoming. When you mature to the point that your internal motivations outweigh your external motivations, you embody the essence of the work ethic. Through the mastery of your soul at work, you discover the path to joy in your work. Character, joy, and work should be familiar bedfellows. And your work should be deeply rewarding.

5

FOR THE LOVE
OF MONEY

We work to become, not to acquire.

ELBERT HUBBARD

D ad believed money would solve all his problems. At 22, so
did I."[1] This quote from a *New York Times Sunday Review*
front page op-ed piece really grabbed my attention. The special
feature gave a firsthand account of Sam Polk, a self-proclaimed
wealth addict. The ambitious young man landed a coveted position on a trading desk with a Wall Street firm upon completing
his undergraduate degree. He chose trading because he wanted to
make as much money as possible, as quickly as possible. He deftly
progressed through the ranks at his first employer and subsequently
took a lucrative trading position at a large hedge fund. Eight years
into his career journey, he had reaped the type of financial rewards
most people only dream about. In what would turn out to be his
final year as a hedge fund trader, he was paid a bonus of $3.6
million. Most would consider this a princely sum for a thirty-year-
old trader. But Sam was furious because he felt he was underpaid.
In just one year, Sam was compensated more than most individuals
earn during their entire working lives . . . and he was angry. This
began a period of deep introspection for Sam. He realized he had

an unhealthy relationship with money and a distorted attitude toward his work. This led to the op-ed feature in the *New York Times* that went viral. I became aware of the article because of the social media chatter. The op-ed piece and later a memoir were both aptly titled, "For the Love of Money."

Sam didn't so much covet the money, but rather what he thought money would provide. From a very young age, he was conditioned to believe money was the cure for his ills and the means to satisfy his cravings. What does Sam's sordid tale have to do with you? After all, a very small percentage of the populace pursues Sam's chosen vocation. Even fewer acquire his level of financial success. However, at the heart of Sam's experience is a quest that is quite common. What is your motivation for your vocational pursuit? What is your attitude toward money? How do those two matters of the heart intersect? Remuneration is generally the first external motivation for work. The desire for monetary reward is universal and evident regardless of the nature of the work or the compensation. It is not so much the money we seek but rather what we believe it will afford us. Many seek the simple peace of mind that comes from receiving a regular paycheck. Financial security, like other forms of safety, is a basic human need. Others covet material possessions. (I have a dear friend who refers to these as our "creature comforts.") For others, it is the power or influence that often accompanies affluence. More than anything, people are seeking true joy. However, the joy people presume money can buy is unavailable for sale. And while you can't buy real joy, you can discover it in your work.

As it turns out, we are not very different from our friend Sam. We must each develop a healthy attitude toward our work, and we must also put our desire for monetary reward in the proper perspective. It is a practical truth that most of us must work to earn a living. The *remuneration* we receive for our work provides for our needs and satisfies our wants. Compensation is only part of the equation; in the long run, it is not even the most important part. We established early on that work produces lasting value to be enjoyed by the wider human community. And while the output of work is valuable, the process of working is equally valuable. Working allows us to realize our God-given abilities and deploy our acquired competencies. Work provides opportunities to collaborate with others, forging meaningful relationships. The true value of the service you render is the work itself. You will never truly derive value from working if you do it simply for the monetary reward. The money will never be enough. Worse still, if you focus on remuneration, your occupation becomes an idol. This improper relationship with your work and your money has a predictable result. You inevitably grow to despise your work because the affirmation you seek comes only from the Creator and not created things.

A mentality that emphasizes working for monetary rewards is based on three common beliefs. The first belief is we should exchange time for money. Most people must work just to make ends meet. In the most basic sense, they offer their ability or time for the opportunity to earn income. As a result, many people live with the constant fear of losing their job. They effectively show up to work hoping they won't be fired. Naturally, they find it difficult to truly enjoy their work. The second belief is we should choose our work based on the level of pay. From an early age, it is impressed upon us that we must obtain a well-paying job. The implication is that a high level of pay will provide financial security and lead to a desirable lifestyle. While high income can lead to an enviable lifestyle in a material sense, it doesn't necessarily lead to a better life. The remuneration offered is one of many considerations and far from the most important when it comes to choosing your work. The third belief is we measure our worth by the size of our bank account. This belief is also often established at an early age. A cultural narrative that suggests a high salary, big house, and fancy car validate success bombards us. Unsurprisingly, many people measure their self-worth by the amount of their financial assets. While these beliefs are fairly common, they are not necessarily universal. As new generational cohorts enter the workplace, we observe some shift in values. My primary point is the aforementioned ways of thinking are neither true nor profitable. A healthy attitude toward work helps put monetary reward in the proper perspective.

TIME VALUE OF MONEY

Henry Ford is counted among a cohort of influential business magnates who were captains of the second industrial revolution. This group included luminaries such as John D. Rockefeller, Andrew Carnegie, and Howard Hughes. The business processes and employment practices they instituted had an enduring impact on workplace culture. Paradoxically, the misapplication of yesteryear's management philosophies often impedes the work ethic. As the saying goes, to everything there is a time and a season (Eccles 3:1-8). In this case, the operative word is *time*. The most common occupations during the second industrial revolution involved manufacturing or working in factories. The basic measure of productivity was output per unit of time. This simple yet enduring rubric still shapes many attitudes regarding work. This is true even though an ever-increasing portion of the workforce is engaged in knowledge work. Many employers and employees alike have adopted a mindset of bartering time for money, becoming materially and morally poorer in the process.

What's wrong with bartering time for money? Isn't that the basic arrangement between employers and workers, after all? This exposes the first commonly held belief: we should exchange time for money. If we link compensation to time expended instead of outcomes achieved, we lose sight of three essential things: the purpose of our work, the process of professional development, and the people we are accountable to. Modern workforce trends offer an extended framework for thinking about time and money. A burgeoning section of the workforce in developed countries participates in what is known as the gig economy. These entrepreneurs and independent contractors exchange goods, services, connections, or know-how for money. While time may not be the principal measure of exchange in the gig economy, money is often the primary motivator. If we lose sight of the purpose, process, and people involved in work, pay is all that remains.

I've come to accept an essential truth as it pertains to this relationship between time and money. Time is a finite and precious resource. No amount of talent or tenacity enables us to extend the 24-hour day. Therefore, we can never truly be compensated for our time. We can assign an hourly wage for a task or assignment. We can similarly set an annual salary for a specialized role. However, these forms of monetary compensation will never be sufficient to engender full engagement. Tomorrow is not promised, which makes every moment of each day precious. In a manner of speaking, your time is priceless. Do we view our workday as time well spent? Do we find lasting value in our overall experience in the workplace?

Work isn't about counting the time but about making the time count. It is essential to view the time we commit to our work as an investment rather than as an exchange. The investment, as opposed to the exchange of time, provides the opportunity to create immeasurable value. The value created is the basis for remuneration and recognition. Moreover, it is the basis for the personal value we place on our contributions in the workplace. A genuine work ethic is exhibited by what we create as opposed to what we consume. Careful stewardship of our time makes our work experience more meaningful.

MONEY AND MEANING

I recently viewed an online presentation that explored what makes us feel good about work.[2] The presenter, Dan Ariely, is a professor of Psychology and Behavioral Economics as well as a bestselling author. His basic premise was to provide evidence that our motivation for work is not solely based on remuneration. This intrigued me because it related to the second commonly held belief: we should choose our work based on the level of pay. His research examined internal motivators for work, one of the most essential being meaningfulness. He first tested his hypothesis by devising an experiment in which two groups were paid to assemble Lego sets. With each assembly, the rate of pay offered was decreased. All the conditions were the same save one. The first group's assembled Lego bricks were stored under the table while the second group's assembled Lego bricks were disassembled immediately upon completion. How did they fare? The second group made seven assemblies on average while the first group pressed on to an average of eleven assemblies. Each group received commensurate pay but produced very different results. Just adding a modest sense of purpose tapped into the internal motivation of meaningfulness.

My earliest admonishments concerning work often sounded like this: "Make sure to do well in school so you can secure a well-paying job." For some of my friends, the advice was, "Pursue an attractive trade so you can secure a well-paying job." For others, it was, "Join the armed forces so you can receive training and development to obtain a well-paying job." Does any of this sound familiar? This was well-intended advice to be sure. It frankly was instrumental in encouraging me along the way. There was, however, a catch. The advice implied one's choice of vocation should be principally based on pay. I would hardly suggest level of pay doesn't matter. It simply isn't *all* that matters, and it is not what matters *most*. As the experiment subtly suggests, we would be much better served choosing meaningful work. I regularly speak with individuals who are seeking to transition to work that is more meaningful but are conflicted by concerns regarding the level of compensation. A dear friend just informed me of his decision to leave what had been a lucrative corporate position for a nonprofit role that offers considerably less pay. Another friend recently shared with me the financial challenges he currently faces having decided to pursue ministry as his full-time occupation, leaving behind a lucrative practice as an attorney. The guideposts are not always clear along our vocational journey. I will offer, however, two helpful pieces of advice to those seeking to discern between different career alternatives. First, choosing work aligned with your interests, abilities, and competencies more readily leads to fit and fulfillment. And second, choosing work that aligns with your sense of purpose is essential for a true work ethic because you are committing to serve the mission and not the money.

WHO WANTS TO BE A MILLIONAIRE?

In 1999, my wife and I lived in an apartment in downtown Chicago. We both worked in office buildings downtown, which made for an easy daily commute. One evening after work I turned on the television as we prepared dinner. I came across a new game show airing in primetime. It was a quiz competition where the contestant answered a series of questions worth specified amounts of money. The questions increased in difficulty along with the prospective prize winnings. If the contestant answered the full series of questions, they took home one million dollars. This was the largest cash prize offered by a game show. The unique format, musical score, and drama contributed to the breakaway success. And while the production was heralded, I believe there was something else at play. In many respects, the name says it all. "Who Wants to Be a Millionaire?" That show, of course, became a cultural phenomenon. I would later learn the US version was not the original. The show first aired in the United Kingdom, offering a top prize of one million pounds. The producers would ultimately spawn numerous international versions airing in 160 countries worldwide. A hallmark of the format was to offer a top prize of one million units of the local currency. It seems this million-dollar question invokes a visceral response. After all, who doesn't want to be a millionaire?

What does a game show have to do with our attitude toward work? Simply put, when it comes to external motivations, money matters. Net worth is defined as the value of everything you own, minus all your debts.[3] Interestingly, the predominant view of personal worth is measured in terms of our financial assets and tangible possessions. This ties to the third and final commonly held belief: we should measure our worth by the amount of our earnings and assets. Practically speaking, your net worth or wealth merely reflects your financial position. This, however, ignores the reality that not everything that counts can be counted. You can't value a person's true worth by assessing their finances. Yet we easily evaluate others and even ourselves based on the money we earn and possessions we accumulate. These become our means of keeping score, our internal assessment of winning or losing in the great race we call life.

This extends to our work lives when we perceive our own value in the workplace as a function of our compensation. A true work ethic espouses just the opposite, disassociating net worth and self-worth. A pure work ethic drives us to create value or wealth to be shared by our community as opposed to possessions to be piled high in our proverbial storehouses. The truest measure of our worth is reflected by what we give as opposed to what we get.

FALSE SECURITY

We began this chapter with the story of ambitious trader Sam. Sam amassed quick riches but soon discovered money alone was an unfulfilling motivation for work. While Sam's life story is very different from my own, we share similar early career experiences. I've spent nearly twenty-five years working in financial services. My interest in finance began at a young age. While other kids dreamed of becoming doctors, lawyers, firefighters, and police officers, I was intrigued by television images of people in suits carrying briefcases. I would tell my mother that was the type of work I would do when I grew up. Later in high school, I took an applied economics course and was introduced to the basic concepts of personal finance, investing, and small business. The simulated real-world applications were intellectually stimulating. I also pursued a unique opportunity to participate in a work-study program where I spent the afternoons of my senior year working in a clerical role for an accounting firm. I enrolled in an undergraduate business program and was on my way to pursuing a career in finance. During college, I had other relevant experiences, including participating in a student-run investment company. The pivotal point came when I was accepted into a scholarship program that included an internship with a prestigious Wall Street firm prior to my senior year. I was the sole intern placed in sales and trading, which was a perfect fit for me. While Wall Street was metaphorically a world away from my childhood home on the Southside of Chicago, I settled in to the fast-paced world of high finance.

I knew little about Wall Street prior to my internship, so the opportunity was serendipitous. I was offered a full-time position following my internship and joined the firm full-time after completing my undergraduate studies. I worked in the sales and trading division, rotating through roles in sales, trading, and research. I will save you the suspense and let you know upfront I neither focused on trading nor subsequently made millions in that line of work as did our friend Sam. I did, however, spend the first eight years of my career working for two prestigious Wall Street firms and completing an MBA at the University of Chicago along the way.

While money was not my sole or principal motivation, my eyes were opened to the role money plays in shaping our attitudes toward work. My parents taught me important lessons about the value and dignity of hard work. I witnessed this firsthand when the Midwest steel mills closed and my father took whatever work was available to make ends meet. It didn't matter if he was cleaning floors or repairing machinery; he took pride in his work. I began taking odd jobs at the age of twelve, including mowing lawns, washing cars, and shoveling snow. My motivation for working wasn't about possessions I coveted but about becoming self-sufficient and doing my part to support our family. I was highly motivated to make a better life for myself and hoped to repay my parents in some way for the many sacrifices they made. I too had to develop the proper attitude regarding work and money. My issue was the perceived security I believed money would afford.

DON'T LET MONEY CHANGE YOU

As I have matured professionally and personally, I've come to see the vital necessity of developing the proper attitude toward work and money. It is impossible to experience true joy in our work if we have an unhealthy relationship with money. Paul the apostle captures the sentiment best in his letter to his protégé Timothy when he profoundly writes that the love of money is the root cause of all kinds of evil (1 Tim 6:10). He went on to observe that people who covet money are burdened with many troubles. This is the opposite of discovering joy in our work. Money is not inherently evil. However, we are susceptible to establishing an unhealthy relationship with it. This extends to our view of monetary rewards derived from work.

Remuneration has its place among our various considerations. It is neither the first consideration nor the most important. A trio of writers picked up on the theme of this unhealthy relationship with money. They put their words to music in a song popularized

by the soul group the O'Jays.[4] They warned that an improper relationship with money could change your mind. When it comes
to work, we must resolve our money issues and our heart issues. As
the O'Jays would say, don't let money change you.

My attitude about money was initially shaped by my childhood
experiences. Money was regularly in short supply. I believed a lucrative career would provide the financial security that seemed so
elusive during my formative years. With wisdom, my attitude has
changed. Sam Polk's story reveals one example of an unhealthy
relationship with money. While Sam sought affluence and an enviable lifestyle, many working people are just trying to get by.
Their experiences may be further challenged by justice issues such
as pay inequality or discriminatory pay practices. Still others may
have a disposition similar to my early attitude toward money. They
seek a sense of security that financial wealth will presumably
provide. Money addresses many of our material needs; however, it
is a resource and not our source. Whether we seek the luxurious
things money can buy or just some peace of mind, remuneration
alone serves as a poor source of motivation. Each of us must put
money in the proper perspective.

The renowned industry titan John D. Rockefeller was well acquainted with producing wealth. It is telling to observe the one
Rockefeller identified as the ultimate source of his wealth and his
personal responsibility considering this truth: "God gave me money.
I believe the power to make money is a gift from God, to be used
and developed to the best of our ability for the best of mankind."[5]
This resonates with my personal pursuits and spiritual beliefs because I believe God indeed gives us the power to create wealth.

Three lessons have helped me on my journey. First, I do not
espouse the belief that work is an exchange of time for money. I've
learned I must provide more service than my pay dictates. While
it is ideal to do work we love, we all can learn to love working and
the simple joy a job well done brings us. Second, I do not espouse

the belief we should choose our work based on the level of pay. I've learned I must serve the mission and not the money. We desire and deserve fair compensation. It is also constructive to have financial goals that relate to our work or vocation. This is most effective when it aligns with our commitment to a shared mission. Finally, I do not espouse the belief our earnings or assets measure our worth. Your current employment situation does not reflect your worth. You are imbued with spiritual wealth that has immeasurable value whether you are currently employed, unemployed, or underemployed.

Putting in place practical disciplines with respect to managing money has been beneficial to my financial and spiritual welfare irrespective of my working situation. When we commit to spending wisely, investing prudently, and giving generously, our money serves us. When the money we earn serves us, we more readily find joy in work. In doing so, we realize our self-worth is far more important than our financial wealth.

For the Love of Money

―――

KEY INSIGHTS

- Remuneration or pay is a primary motivation for work. But monetary reward is insufficient.

- When money serves you, you can more freely serve the mission. Develop the proper relationship with money to discover true joy in work.

- Time is priceless and real work makes time count. Invest time rather than exchanging it.

- Choose your occupation: choose work that aligns with your interests, abilities, and competencies.

- Learn to love your work and the simple joy that comes from a job done well.

- Your health and self-worth are far more important than your financial wealth.

- A pure work ethic drives you to share wealth as opposed to amass possessions. True worth is measured by what you give as opposed to what you get.

6

FOR THE PRAISE
OF PEOPLE

Every master has his true and certain value.
Praise and criticism cannot change any of that. Only
the work itself praises and criticizes the master, and
therefore I leave to everyone his own value.

CARL PHILIPP EMANUEL BACH

One of my favorite family activities is family movie night, and many of my fondest memories involve family outings to watch animated films. My two teenage sons have largely transitioned to other genres of film, but I still have the memories. There is something special about the wonder and imagination experienced through the eyes of a child when viewing an animated film. The experience also gives adults temporary leave to become like kids again, if only for a short spell. While the visual and technical aspects of modern-day film animation are fascinating, the engrossing plots and memorable characters truly bring the tales to life. The masterful storytellers weave engaging narratives that appeal to the entire family. They create evocative characters who make us smile, laugh, and cry. The most remarkable films entertain us while imparting valuable life lessons. About nine years ago, my wife and I had one such experience with our sons. We took our children to see the computer-animated comedy *Despicable Me*. The film had received mixed reviews from critics. My contrarian viewpoint has enabled me to discover some deep truths in unexpected places on the road of life. In this case, I enjoyed some laughs along the way.

Felonius Gru is the protagonist of the story and the main character of the film. Gru is a highly intelligent middle-aged man who is quite inventive. He has, however, taken on a disreputable line of work. Instead of using his talents for good, he is a notorious supervillain. We learn from his backstory that his childhood dream was to become an astronaut and fly to the moon. Unfortunately, others—most notably his mother—disparaged his dreams. So Gru, a promising and inventive young man, goes down a very different path. Gru throws himself into his villainous work. He is praised and followed by his minions and is infamous because of his dastardly deeds. Despite his infamy, Gru is deeply insecure, constantly comparing himself to other villains. (It just goes to show, insecurity is detrimental in any line of work.) His ego becomes particularly bruised when a new supervillain arrives on the scene, stealing the limelight. The pivotal point of the story comes when he adopts three orphaned girls in a devious plot to upstage his challenger. Gru has no intent of keeping the girls, yet something quite unexpected, almost divine, happens to him. The girls see something in Gru he would have never imagined in himself. They see him with the potential to be a loving father. The way these orphaned girls see him ultimately changes the way he views his work and his values.

If you have kids, or you are a kid at heart, you too may have enjoyed *Despicable Me*. If you've ever felt underappreciated or overlooked for your work, you can also relate to the film's leading character, Felonius Gru, whose issues had little to do with the distinctiveness of his work, notwithstanding his dubious profession. He received ample acknowledgement and praise despite his deep insecurity. The heart of the issue was a vocational choice incongruent with his true passion and purpose. He forsook his dreams, becoming a slave to the opinions of others and his own inflated ego. He failed to use his ingenuity to serve others and valued fame rather than a true work ethic. The more he immersed himself into his villainous work, the more he lost touch with his internal motivation and purpose. This invariably fueled his insecurity and constant need for the approval of others. Outwardly, he relished praise, but inwardly he despised his work and by extension the character he'd become. It could be said we should be careful not to let money *or* praise change our character or values.

THE POWER OF PRAISE

How much do we have in common with an animated film character? Likely more than we care to admit. Just like our animated friend, we are invariably motivated by *recognition*, or the praise of others. Praise is an expression of acceptance, approval, or admiration of someone or something done. We feel a special sense of affirmation when others express a good opinion of our work. If work were a performance art, we would observe people perform for both money and praise. In certain instances, praise provides greater motivation than money. We live in an age where common measures of success include posts, likes, and followers. This highlights the fact that people place an outsized value on praise. This attitude is regularly on display in the workplace. To be clear, there is nothing inherently wrong with sincere praise. Furthermore, it is considerate and appropriate to recognize individuals for work done well. However, if praise is the principal motivation for our work, much is lost in the process. First, we run the risk of robbing others of the lasting value our effort can produce. It is the product and not the praise that results in value. Second, we run the risk of robbing ourselves of the opportunity to build our character through our work. This is the essence of a genuine work ethic.

I recently had an experience that illuminates the power of praise. Christmas is a very special time of year for our family. We engage in meaningful expressions of our faith and acts of generosity. My sons decided to put their talents to good use by making several of their gifts. My eldest son, who shares my love for writing, created a devotional guide for his mother. My younger son, who is artistically inclined, sketched a portrait of my sister's family. I was unaware of their gift ideas and was surprised when they gave me a preview of them. I complimented them on the exceptional quality of their work. I also expressed my appreciation for their thoughtfulness and creativity. My sons were both beaming with pride, and so was their proud father. This was not an ostentatious show of egotism or exaggerated self-esteem. Their response was an expression of delight brought about by my positive affirmation. It occurred to me they experienced the joy that comes from work done well. The motivation for their work was not self-centered, and they were not seeking remuneration or recognition. As such, their response was pure and genuine. The praise I offered gave greater meaning to their work and boosted their self-esteem.

Praise is an expression of support or encouragement, expressed in three forms: *acceptance*, *approval*, and *admiration*. Each form reveals unique aspects of praise and helps us better understand our true motivations. Acceptance, the first expression of praise, is the most fundamental. We work and live in community and everything we do has a relational impact. Beyond a means of earning a living, our work represents our offering to the Creator and all of creation. When we offer our talent in the form of work, we naturally want the output to be acknowledged and accepted. Approval is the second expression of praise. As it pertains to our work, it arguably is the most prevalent. Though related, approval connotes something different from acceptance. Approval affirms that the work meets or exceeds a clear standard. It means the work is suitable for the intended purpose and a satisfactory opinion is conferred upon our effort. Admiration is the third expression of praise, and it is particularly coveted by certain personality types. When others admire our work, it evokes a deep emotional response. The pride and joy we feel as the creator of the work is passed on to the beneficiary. Each expression of praise is valuable and serves as an extrinsic reward for work.

With my sons, I realized all three expressions of praise were at play in our interaction. What's more, our respective responses provide several lessons on the power of praise. In each instance, my boys took a degree of risk with their gift ideas. They applied their unique talents, which required a more substantial investment of time and effort. The first message my praise connoted was acceptance. I acknowledged their hard work and gave them confidence their gifts would be warmly greeted by the intended recipients. The second message my praise connoted was approval. I am the primary role model for my sons. They look to me for approval that their work and behavior meet and exceed expectations. My words serve as a vital source of affirmation that their work and work ethic are good. The third and final message my praise connoted was admiration. It was apparent I held their work in especially high regard. The pride and joy they felt in creating the work were matched by the pride and joy I felt in seeing their workmanship. I praised their work despite the fact they were not seeking praise. Praise unquestionably serves as a strong source of encouragement and motivation. Praise diminishes in value when we outwardly seek it but is of lasting value when it results from a true work ethic.

CONSTRUCTIVE CRITICISM

While praise is a desired form of recognition, we must be prepared for the opposite response. We learn from a very young age that work invites both praise and criticism. Like praise, criticism is a form of expression. More specifically, it is an assessment, judgment, or evaluation of someone or something. The term *criticism* generally has a negative connotation, as it is most regularly defined as an expression of disapproval. However, criticism is not necessarily synonymous with disapproval. It is, however, true that those critiques of our work reveal perceived faults, flaws, or mistakes. These opinions may be associated with the output of our work or the way we work. Because we are affected by the opinions of others, the feelings evoked are generally opposite of what we feel when our work is praised. The very nature of work subjects our efforts to continuous scrutiny and appraisal. We have standards by which we are measured and objectives we must meet or exceed. Criticism of our work is not only common, it is inevitable. Therefore, organizations extol the virtues of giving and receiving criticism constructively. The way we express feedback to and receive feedback from others impacts our attitude toward work. In the end, praise cannot serve as our principal motivator, and criticism cannot become a principal detractor from a genuine work ethic.

A clear understanding of each unique expression of criticism can help us to give and receive criticism more constructively. *Assessment*, the first expression of criticism, is the most fundamental. Work is performed with an audience or recipient in mind. We endeavor to deliver a product or service acceptable to the customer or client. An assessment of our work product affirms both its authenticity and its utility. A proper assessment ensures the work product is appropriate for the intended recipient. *Judgment* is the second expression of criticism. As it pertains to our work, it is usually the most prevalent. Our work is regularly measured against implicit and explicit objectives. In many instances, our work must be critically investigated for flaws or mistakes to ensure the best possible results. This ensures that the quality of the present workmanship meets or exceeds reasonably established standards while allowing for continuous improvement in the future. *Evaluation* is the third expression of criticism and is the most comprehensive. A comprehensive evaluation speaks to the value of our work product as compared to expectations and similar products. When our work is evaluated, an opinion of the overall merit is conferred. A favorable evaluation of our work boosts our self-confidence, which drives our desire for recognition.

When it comes to our work, criticism can demotivate us. This is especially true if we are expecting or seeking praise. Yet criticism can prove useful if given and received in the proper way. Constructive criticism serves as valuable feedback that helps us grow professionally and personally—the operative word being *constructive*. One of my primary executive responsibilities is to provide talented individuals with regular feedback and coaching. This is as much art as it is science. I recently enjoyed a very productive conversation with a senior leader that reinforced what it looks like when feedback is given and received effectively. David is a talented executive I personally recruited to join our team. While much of the early feedback from his peers was positive, a particular theme emerged regarding his style of engagement. David is exceptionally insightful and highly inquisitive. Though sociable, he is a natural introvert. Some of his peers perceived him as aloof and critical. I believed David would make appropriate adjustments with the benefit of proactive feedback and coaching.

The first key to providing constructive feedback is preparation. These are crucial conversations that must be handled with care. Your good intentions must be clear. I took the time to write down my key messages prior to our meeting.

"David, may I offer you some feedback based on observations from your colleagues?" I asked.

"Of course, you can," David replied. It was clear from David's response and demeanor that he was open to the dialogue.

"The general feedback is quite positive. However, you have an opportunity to enhance your effectiveness," I offered.

This brings me to the second key to providing constructive feedback. Proceed with caution! In our eagerness to give people a piece of our mind, we often raise their defenses. Feedback is not particularly helpful if the recipient is unreceptive. We must patiently listen with our head and our heart if we seek to have a positive impact. Finally, it is important to give specifics. Identify specific behaviors or actions to be addressed. Provide specific advice on correctives as appropriate.

My specific advice to David was to spend more time with colleagues outside of formal meetings. This would allow him to better understand his audience and increase his relationship capital with team members. David offered two simple words at the conclusion of our dialogue. "Thank you," he said with a smile. David responded favorably, strengthening his relationships with colleagues and enhancing his leadership effectiveness.

One of the ways we can positively contribute to the communities in which we work is by using our words wisely. As the adage goes, "Words shape worlds." More to the point, an essential area of personal and professional growth for most individuals involves receptivity to feedback. This is certainly an area of continued focus for me. While most of us view ourselves as open and curious, research and practical observation reveal we have significant room for growth in seeking and applying feedback. Even our explicit requests for feedback can be veiled solicitations for praise as we seek recognition. Here again, the work ethic comes into play. If we are motivated by a genuine work ethic, we can extract all useful observations from feedback that can help us improve our work product. All feedback, critical or otherwise, has value. It provides us with insight into people's perceptions of our work style and our work product. Whether the feedback comes in the form of praise or criticism, it has the potential to provide valuable lessons. In the long run, it matters less if the feedback we get is delivered constructively. The key to personal and professional growth is receiving criticism constructively.

REDO YOUR PERFORMANCE REVIEW

The most familiar critique offered in formal work settings arrives in the form of the annual performance review. Performance reviews are intended to provide us with actionable feedback regarding the quality of our work as well as our effectiveness working with others. In the purest sense, the objective is to increase our productivity and develop our career potential. Good intentions notwithstanding, this annual ritual often results in a destructive rather than constructive form of criticism. This is not to say managers are intentionally callous in their critiques. Many managers dread giving performance appraisals and are often ill-prepared to do so. More often than not, their feedback simply misses the mark with respect to encouraging a genuine work ethic. Whether their criticism is too vague, too biased, too sterile, or just too late, the developmental value of the appraisal is often squandered. Subordinates, for their part, are often ill-tempered and ill-prepared to listen to candid feedback. Most individuals are defensive, resisting even gentle critiques. Anything short of high praise is often met with dejection or resentment. It turns out the effects of criticism rival the power of praise. Whether words of praise or criticism, people take it personally. Constant criticism is equally detrimental to both the giver and the recipient.

Have you ever had a poor performance review? I recall a particularly challenging performance review and the lessons I learned from that experience. In hindsight, the evaluation was benign, and my overall rating was positive. However, I received an unsatisfactory rating in effective communication. The rating and associated feedback came as a surprise because I hadn't perceived a developmental need. The business unit I managed had posted strong financial results, and I had successfully assumed additional management responsibilities. I expected these achievements to be the highlight of my performance review. Instead my manager focused on what he identified as a tendency to over communicate.

He observed that this limited my effectiveness at times. We spent the balance of the review discussing his developmental feedback.

The reason this was a challenging performance review had little to do with the nature of the feedback. The review was challenging because I wasn't mentally prepared to receive the critique of my work. Let's be honest. It isn't easy to absorb negative feedback or criticism. Unsurprisingly, my initial response was defensive. However, after a bit of reflection and wise counsel, I turned the feedback into a genuine growth opportunity.

So how did I recover from my initial setback? The first step was to reframe the feedback I received. A mentor once encouraged me to treat all feedback as a gift. I was confident my manager and other senior leaders were committed to my professional development and career success. A common workplace challenge is the lack of candid feedback. My manager felt comfortable providing frank and specific feedback because of our rapport. Upon reflection, this was indeed a gift. In my dialogues with executive management, I was spending too much time on context. This unwittingly suggested I was not fully in tune with my audience. In general, I needed to be more concise in my communications with fellow executives. This would offer clearer insights and ensure my message was not lost in verbiage.

After processing the feedback, which included getting counsel from a trusted mentor, I followed up in writing with my manager. I began by providing a written summary of my takeaways and proposed action plan. We also agreed to discuss developmental progress at regularly scheduled intervals. There were three valuable things that happened because of my recovery plan. First, I grew professionally and personally with respect to this core competency. There was, in fact, plenty of room for improvement. Second, I enhanced my relationship with my manager, resulting in more timely and actionable feedback. Finally, I have become more adept at receiving criticism constructively, though I am admittedly a work in progress.

Considering my experience, I offer the following advice for maximizing the value of performance feedback. The first piece of advice is simple but not easy: listen carefully and objectively to feedback. If you begin with the perspective that something of value will be conveyed, then you are well on your way to improving the quality of your work. The second piece of advice is to demonstrate a positive attitude. If you place yourself in the shoes of the giver, you understand their position is equally challenging. It's not easy to give constructive feedback. Since you are the ultimate beneficiary, you make the giver's job easier if you remain open and curious. The third piece of advice is to identify at least one near-term action step. Acting on the feedback makes you more likely to appreciate it and grow from it, particularly when you experience positive results from applying what you've learned. Finally, you should seek opportunities to pay it forward. You really do reap what you sow. If you provide others with thoughtful, honest feedback regarding their work, two things are likely to happen. You will enhance your relationships with coworkers and more readily get the feedback you need to grow professionally. With the proper work ethic, you can translate criticism into work worthy of praise.

Carl Philipp Emanuel Bach, musician and composer, was the second surviving son of the renowned composer Johann Sebastian Bach.[1] His older brother, Johann Christian Bach, served as music master to the Queen of England. Talk about your tough acts to follow. My guess is the younger Bach experienced his fair share of both praise and criticism of his work. Emanuel, as his associates knew him, became a very influential composer in his own right. His dedication to his craft provided him with a unique perspective of work and the work ethic. He offered this valuable insight. "Every master has his true and certain value. Praise and criticism cannot change any of that. Only the work itself praises and criticizes the master, and therefore I leave to everyone his own value."[2]

It seems Emanuel developed a pure work ethic. He was not unduly motivated by praise nor dissuaded by criticism. It was the work, in and of itself, that motivated him. It wasn't his father's praise, his brother's praise, or any other individual's praise that drove him to produce great compositions. While he appreciated recognition as a form of reward, it was the quality of his work that spoke to him and for him. The lesson we learn from his insight is clear. Instead of seeking praise for our work, we should commit ourselves to workmanship that is praiseworthy. This type of work ethic produces stellar work and lasting joy.

For the Praise of People

———

KEY INSIGHTS

- Recognition or praise is another motivation for work. Recognition serves as an expression of acceptance, approval, or admiration.

- Balance the desire for recognition with healthy personal values.

- Recognition diminishes in value when you outwardly seek it, but it is of lasting value when it results from a true work ethic.

- Work is subject to continuous scrutiny and appraisal; criticism is not only common, it is inevitable.

- All feedback, critical or positive, has value. It provides insight into people's perceptions of your work style and product.

- Listen carefully and objectively to feedback. Expect something of value to be conveyed.

- Commit to workmanship that is praiseworthy versus seeking praise for work.

7

FOR THE
PRIDE OF LIFE

When your work speaks for itself,
don't interrupt.

HENRY J. KAISER

P eople take great pride in their work. The famous songstress
Aretha Franklin comes to mind as she brazenly declared,
"R-E-S-P-E-C-T, find out what it means to me." And lest my
readers presume the popular song is solely a female anthem, I
would point out the lesser-known fact that Otis Redding originally
released it two years prior.[1] Men and women alike have an inherent
need to be respected for their contributions and achievements.

This is particularly true when it comes to our work and vocational pursuits. An inherent feeling of satisfaction accompanies
finishing a difficult task or completing a meaningful assignment.
This is because our ego is figuratively and literally invested in our
work. *Ego*, which is Latin for "I," is the part of our psyche that
experiences and reacts to the outside world. Our self-esteem is
affected by the value placed on our work. When others value our
work, it lifts our self-esteem. Criticism of our work has the opposite effect. It matters that we receive *respect* for our work. The
fact that our work matters to us is a good thing. Good work is,

indeed, something we should be proud of. As with most things, though, it is important to keep pride in the proper perspective.

Pride is an attitude of the mind. There are two common definitions for *pride* that have very different connotations. The first definition of *pride* refers to a feeling of pleasure you get because you or someone you are closely connected with does something good. This positive connotation associated with achievement is also tempered by humility. There is a second definition of *pride*, which has a negative connotation and refers to a high or exaggerated opinion of one's importance or achievements. This selfish type of pride is typified by a lack of humility. Our feelings about our vocational abilities, accomplishments, and achievements can lead to positive or negative expressions of pride. There is a thin line between these two contrasting expressions. Exhibiting the type of work ethic that keeps us firmly on the right side of the line is essential to discovering joy in our work.

TIME FOR A PROMOTION

Several years ago, I had a dinner conversation with my family that reinforced our constant need to manage the emotion of pride with the spirit of humility. It was the early part of the year, which was a particularly busy time for me professionally. As a general manager with bottom line accountability, a variety of urgent matters typically arise at the start of a new year. The days often feel like a series of sprints during those periods. During one of those busy days, I received some terrific news from my manager, a member of the company's executive management committee. He stopped by my office to inform me that the board of directors had approved my promotion to executive vice president. My company, like other corporations, confers official titles that denote one's level of seniority within the company. The official title is also a designation that signifies a level of respect or regard for cumulative contributions to the enterprise. Beginning with the first designation of officer, an employee can be promoted based on ongoing assessments of performance. The title of executive vice president is a highly coveted title and one of the highest distinctions conferred in our firm. Forty-five of the approximately fifteen thousand employees held the designation at the time.

I felt a strong sense of pride when I received word of my promotion. It showed respect for my contributions to the organization and a reflection of how my work was viewed by my superiors; it was effectively a show of respect for my work. I paused and phoned my wife to share the news, turning quickly again to the pressing matters of the day. When I arrived home late that evening, my wife and two sons were still at the dinner table. Although they had finished, they patiently waited to ensure I received a warm welcome. My sons, who were ten and twelve years of age at the time, didn't know much about corporate culture. They also paid no mind to professional titles. They did, however, know they had hard working parents, and they surmised a promotion was surely a good thing. My wife had previously worked in a management role for a leading consulting firm. She knew all too well the demands of the corporate world and the enduring challenges of the workplace. While my wife had a natural appreciation for this recent accomplishment, my sons were interested in getting a better understanding of what it meant.

As I began my supper, my eldest son began the inquiry. He specifically wanted to understand why I was promoted. He is an abstract thinker like his father and is naturally drawn to questions of why. Though not an exact science, exceptional performance and the proven facility to work well with others are generally prerequisites for promotion. I explained my promotion reflected the value placed on the service I render to coworkers and clients. He was reasonably satisfied with my response. My younger son is highly analytical and a concrete communicator in the mold of his mother. He was interested to understand the practical changes that would come because of my promotion. He proceeded to ask a series of questions: "Are you moving to a new office? Will you be working with different people? Are you getting a new boss? Do you have different responsibilities? Are you making more money?" He was surprised to find the answer to each of these questions was no. Clearly perplexed he asked, "What does promotion mean at your company?" It was an innocent yet insightful question. What does a promotion really mean?

As the words settled, I realized his final question was very profound. From his vantage point, no practical changes resulted from my promotion. The change in title was very meaningful in one context and had little meaning in a different context. His question encouraged some healthy introspection on my part. The promotion was a commendation of my work and an important milestone in my career progression. It was genuinely something to be proud of. This form of respect is a familiar source of motivation that fosters our work effort. Like any externally driven motivation, it must be kept in the proper context. We must be careful not to unduly tie our self-worth to our position or the esteem in which others hold us. I can readily admit that promotion matters as it relates to my work. The concern is not whether it matters, but rather whether it matters too much. There is a selfish form of pride that can arise in relation to our professional contributions, status, or accomplishments. This kind of pride or self-promotion presages professional and personal failures.

Transforming your occupation into your vocation requires you to rise above selfish ambition. Again, it entails maturing mentally and spiritually to the point that your motivation for work originates from within. This selfless brand of promotion is essential to discovering joy in your work.

LET YOUR WORK DO THE TALKING

Henry Kaiser was an industrialist who is widely regarded as the father of modern shipbuilding. He not only famously built ships during World War II, but he was responsible for many commercial enterprises that bear his namesake.[2] He formed Kaiser Aluminum, Kaiser Steel, Kaiser Motors, and Kaiser Permanente, which provided health care for his workers and their families. Kaiser, the son of ethnic German immigrants, rose from humble beginnings by means of his strong work ethic and entrepreneurial spirit. The broader impact of his life's work extended beyond the enterprises he founded. His work and entrepreneurism were instrumental in the development and prosperity of the American West. His involvement in the construction of civic centers, schools, roads, and dams is a lasting testament to his work contributions. He also used his wealth to establish the Kaiser Family Foundation, which focuses on health issues. Despite his many contributions, he is remembered as a pragmatic man who did not seek the limelight. His attitude toward work is best exemplified by a simple quote: "When your work speaks for itself, don't interrupt." In other words, he did not demand respect, but rather his work commanded respect.

When we consider the words and deeds of Henry Kaiser, it is apparent he took great pride in his work. He experienced joy derived from his many professional achievements, and the value of his work spoke on his behalf. In fact, his work continues to speak to future generations. People with a genuine work ethic feel no compulsion to brag or behave in a way that puffs up their ego. They recognize pride in one's work differs from pride in one's self. This type of humility starkly contrasts what we commonly observe and even our own inclination at times. We are regularly encouraged to promote our personal brand, raise our professional profile, and highlight our vocational achievements, all in the name of career success. The way we see ourselves relative to our coworkers unconsciously becomes a primary focus. Our work is connected to our selfhood, and we want respect. This generally results in a tendency to exaggerate our position or contributions relative to others. The wisdom of Henry Kaiser's words becomes even more apparent. We are most productive and most fulfilled when we simply allow our work to speak for itself. This disposition earns the respect of others and helps guard our heart against selfish pride.

WHO GETS THE CREDIT?

One form of pride is synonymous with hubris or lack of humility. This attitude of the heart, which differs from pride in our work, is evidenced when we seek to advance or exaggerate our position relative to others. This attitude impairs our ability to do good work and adversely affects our relationships with others. This self-centered form of pride is most commonly typified by four distinct behaviors: *presumption*, *boastfulness*, *arrogance*, and *ostentation*. Each of these behaviors results from an unhealthy relationship with our work. We too often focus on looking good as opposed to doing good.

There is a basic litmus test for distinguishing pride in our work from selfish pride: Who gets the credit? This simple question reveals a great deal about our true motives. Are we principally concerned with the degree to which we are acknowledged for the work we perform? Are we envious of others who are recognized for their work? Do we praise coworkers for shared successes? Do we readily accept accountability for our mistakes or failures? Do we disparage the work of others to exalt our own work? I can admit to instances when I have been inordinately concerned with who gets the credit. This type of self-interest deprives us of the true joy to be experienced in our work.

Work ethic reflects the belief that our vocation is instrumental in building our character. A genuine work ethic is exemplified by the quality of humility—having a modest opinion of one's own self-importance. It is exemplified by being courteous and respectful to others as opposed to demanding respect. A humble person does not suffer from low self-esteem—quite the contrary. A humble person has a healthy self-esteem. This enables the individual to pursue the moral benefits of work and not simply personal gain. Selfish pride is antithetical to this mindset because it is fueled by an undue emphasis on the external motivation of respect. Our opinion of our position relative to others matters too much to us. This preoccupation with our position takes our focus away from our work and erodes the qualities of the work ethic. Moreover, this mindset leads to *presumptuous, boastful, arrogant,* or *ostentatious* behaviors. It would be convenient to ignore a consideration of these behaviors save the sobering reality we are all susceptible to them. Martin Luther King Jr. spoke rightly when he said, "There is some good in the worst of us and some evil in the best of us."[3] We will examine the root causes of selfish pride and learn how a true work ethic guards against its manifestations.

ADDRESSING BAD BEHAVIORS

Presumption. Presumption, which is often marked by over-stepping proper bounds, is associated with self-centered pride. It is synonymous with forward or overconfident behaviors. Presumptuous behavior can even be well-intentioned but betray an inflated sense of one's own importance. Assuming authority in the boss's absence when unwarranted is an example of presumption. Exaggerating your own contributions in relation to those of co-workers is another example of presumptuous behavior. Our thirst for glory reveals a lack of respect for other people. This type of behavior devalues our work. Understanding the root cause holds the key to guarding against this behavior.

Since the impetus for presumption is to take credit from others, we do well to practice the opposite. A wise man once told me we each have lights intended to shine brightly. The question is whether we choose to shine like a moon or a star. He preferred a moon because it shines by reflecting light. As it applies to our work, the message is clear. Most of our work is done in collaboration with others. Therefore, we should be quick to credit others and recognize their work. By so doing, we cultivate a genuine work ethic and discover joy in our work.

Boastfulness. Boastfulness is another behavior associated with self-centered pride. Taking excessive pride in one's abilities or achievements marks boastfulness. This behavior is primarily revealed by what we say. As the proverb says, from the abundance of the heart, the mouth speaks (Lk 6:45). Boastful individuals talk about their ability and their work in a self-admiring way. This prideful form of speaking may begin with meritorious claims but often lead to excessive or embellished assertions. The desire for others to hold us in excess esteem leads to boastfulness. You've undoubtedly encountered someone you've considered boastful. What did you think of that person? What impression do we make when we exhibit similar behaviors? This type of immodesty reveals a lack of self-awareness. It is utterly opposed to Henry Kaiser's admonishment to let our work do the talking.

Understanding the root cause of this behavior helps us guard against it. Since it stems from the desire to be held in excess esteem, the antidote is obvious: we must esteem our coworkers highly. In fact, I argue we should concern ourselves more with the well-being of our coworkers and be less concerned with our own standing. Work is much more enjoyable when we learn to care about ourselves less. This too is one of the secrets to discovering joy in our work.

Arrogance. Arrogance is marked by an overbearing manner and offensive displays of self-importance. Arrogant behavior reflects an attitude of superiority that comes from a belief we are smarter, better, or more important than our coworkers. This is not simply an insulting way of thinking; it is an insulting way of being. By that, I refer to both conscious and unconscious actions aimed at those around us. The desire to feel more important or more valued than our coworkers leads to arrogance. And while we rightly associate arrogance with an undue sense of self-confidence, it ultimately reveals an unhealthy sense of self-esteem.

Again, guarding against this type of behavior is tied to our ability to uncover the root cause. My father taught me a great deal about work and life. He would often say that comparison breeds discontentment. I am regularly reminded of this prescient observation as I navigate my professional career. Too often we rob ourselves of the delight in our work by comparing ourselves to others. The key to guarding against arrogance is learning to chart and complete our own course. We do not discover joy in our work by making it comparatively better. It is discovered by making our work the best it can be. We further guard against arrogance by demonstrating our appreciation for the work of others. Arrogance and appreciation cannot occupy the same mental space.

Ostentation. Ostentation is the final behavior I associate with selfish pride. It is exhibited through pretentious or vainglorious displays intended to attract attention. Ostentatious behavior reflects an inordinate need for external validation. And while most expressions of prideful behavior betray self-centered motives, ostentation is arguably the most pronounced. The desire to have positions of power over others to inflate our ego leads to ostentation. This desire reflects both a high degree of insecurity and a low level of empathy. Ostentatious behavior is a power play with the goal of usurping authority. This aggressive posture leads to conflict with coworkers.

Just as before, understanding the root cause of this behavior helps us put appropriate safeguards in place. The key to guarding against ostentation is what I refer to as the "Superman principle." This fictional character is imbued with superhuman abilities and a strong moral compass. Rather than seek a position of power over others, he humbly assumes the identity of Clark Kent. The mild-mannered reporter eschews ostentatious displays all the while protecting humanity through his alternate identity, Superman. Each of us is imbued with God-given abilities and must similarly use our powers for good. Again, we must focus on doing good as opposed to looking good. Empowering others exemplifies a true work ethic and is a sure path to discovering joy in our work.

FEELING INFLATED?

You are likely familiar with the proverbial expression that a little leaven leavens the whole lump (Gal 5:9). Leaven is a substance, usually yeast, which causes dough to ferment and rise. Metaphorically, it describes a pervasive influence that alters or changes someone or something. This metaphor is a fitting simile for selfish pride, which engenders an inflated opinion of one's position or abilities. The slightest hint of this type of attitude can negatively impact your work. A brief science lesson on yeast is quite instructive. Microscopic yeasts are present in the air all around you yet are undetectable to your natural senses. These airborne elements will organically cling to a mixture of dough under most atmospheric conditions. Once the leaven is added, fermenting or puffing up will occur naturally. Selfish pride works in much the same way. The external stimuli that lead to selfish desires and prideful behavior are all around you.

"I'm not sure what came over you in that meeting today, but I frankly thought you were condescending," Stan said sternly. As I stared at him in disbelief, I quickly replayed the earlier meeting in my mind. What had I missed? I had recently assumed a role managing the firm's brokerage business. A major part of my responsibilities involved working with several business unit leaders to deliver brokerage services to their clients. Several of my team members were unhappy with the way our services were marketed to clients. In short, they felt we should have been a higher priority. I shared their sentiment and felt pressured to assert our view. This is just the type of stimuli that leads to an unhealthy form of pride. Stan was a highly respected executive who employed a quiet style of leadership. Stan had also become a dear friend to me. As such, his rebuke really got my attention.

After a long pause, I looked at Stan earnestly and said, "I apologize." It was the only reasonable response. After further reflection, my blind spot came into clear view. The substance of my message wasn't the issue. My inflated ego was the problem. A little leaven does indeed leaven the lump. The next day I personally apologized to each executive that attended the meeting. It was a humbling experience that left a lasting impression.

Remember, pride is not inherently bad as it pertains to work. However, our attitude and behavior must be critically examined to ensure our motives are pure. A healthy degree of self-respect removes the inclination to demand respect from your coworkers. Likewise, recognizing the contributions of coworkers, and making sure others see them, puts our own work in the proper perspective. Guarding your heart against selfish pride allows your true work ethic to shine through. This leads to contentment in your position and joy in your work.

CHAPTER 7 REFLECTIONS

For the Pride of Life

KEY INSIGHTS

- Respect is another primary motivation for work. You must, however, be careful to act with humility because your ego is invested in your work.

- Satisfaction is derived from finishing a difficult task or completing a meaningful assignment.

- When your motivation for work originates from within, you begin to transform your occupation into your vocation.

- Selfishly seeking to advance your position impairs your ability to do good work and adversely affects your relationships with others.

- Don't care who gets the credit. Be quick to credit others and recognize their work.

- Maintain a modest opinion of your own self-importance and be courteous to others.

- Allow your work to speak for itself. Work becomes more enjoyable as you learn to care less about yourself.

PART THREE

YOUR
WORK LIFE

Your work is going to fill a large part of your life,
and the only way to be truly satisfied is to do what you
believe is great work. And the only way to do
great work is to love what you do.

STEVE JOBS

I recently read a very interesting article in the *New York Times Sunday Review*. The title of the article was "Why Succeeding Against the Odds Can Make You Sick."[1] The article highlighted a body of research that reveals the surprising negative health effects linked to upward mobility. The research involved examining the socioeconomic backgrounds and personalities of an identified group of subjects referred to as "strivers." These individuals shared a trait known in psychology as resilience. They were very adept at setting goals and working diligently to achieve them. They didn't simply work hard but rather cultivated the quality of persistence. Moreover, they possessed a distinct ability to achieve in the face of difficult circumstances, leading to professional and financial success. Their high achievement apparently came at a substantive cost. Conventional wisdom suggested as their socioeconomic status improved, so too would their health. However, the research results revealed a curious pattern. The subjects who tended to strive more for success were also more likely to encounter health problems. The implication of the research is the health of the "striver" suffers even as he or she perseveres in the face of adversity. I pondered the inferences this hypothesis might also suggest for discovering joy in our work.

As the researchers delved further, they uncovered particularly interesting findings related to African American subjects from disadvantaged backgrounds. Even when controlling for other factors, their resiliency in the face of certain obstacles appeared to be accompanied by ailments including diabetes, hypertension, and low white blood cell counts. This pattern was not found with white persons from similar circumstances. In fact, certain health problems acute among African Americans are not exhibited in blacks from other countries. One of the subjects, John Henry Martin, was born into a family of sharecroppers. John worked tirelessly to escape this system and by the age of forty, owned seventy-five acres of farmland. Over the ensuing decade, John suffered from hypertension, arthritis, and a host of other health-related ailments. This led one of the researchers to name the effect "John Henryism" based on his plight as well as the legendary figure bearing the same name. While the name of the effect was assumed to be associated discreetly with African American men, this was neither the expectation nor the aim of the research. Regardless of race, gender, or socioeconomic status, the high-effort coping we experience in our work lives impacts each of us. Our work matters in the context of our life.

YOU ARE LEGEND

For those who may be unfamiliar, John Henry is an African American folk hero with an all-too-American story.[2] He was born a slave but later became a free man. He was said to stand six feet tall and weigh two hundred pounds, a very striking figure during his time. Henry utilized his physical prowess to become a steel driver. Railroad companies hired by the thousands for tasks such as smoothing out terrain and cutting through obstacles that stood in the proposed path of the tracks. Steel drivers used large hammers and stakes to pound holes into the rock, which were then filled with explosives. Only the strongest, most determined workers were cut out for this arduous task. Henry was exceptional at the task, regularly completing a workload of three or more men in a day. When railroad companies began to employ steam drills to power holes into the rock, the livelihood of Henry and his fellow laborers was threatened. According to legend, Henry challenged the steam-powered hammer to a contest. Henry bested the steam-powered machine, winning by a substantial margin. Henry, however, paid the ultimate price for his effort, dying with his hammer in his hands. Some accounts say he died due to an aneurysm in his brain while other accounts say his heart gave out. Either way, his superhuman effort resulted in his untimely and unfortunate death. His legend offers lessons of reflection for workers of all creeds and circumstances.

What does the legend of John Henry teach us? Let's begin with a fundamental truth. Work is a vital part of our human experience. It demands substantial time, effort, and energy and challenges us physically, mentally, and spiritually. However, we must not allow our work to consume our lives. Our work is intended to fit in the context of our lives and not the other way around. Work done well brings us joy and not sorrow. We all can relate to the story of John Henry regardless of our race, gender, or background. We strive diligently to achieve success in our work. The associated stress and the demands, some of which are self-imposed, cause disharmony in our lives.

We struggle to obtain the elusive goal of work-life balance. And while this concept is often deliberated, I submit the more apt objective is "work-life synergy." Your work must be properly integrated into your life. It's less about balancing opposing sides of a scale and more about fitting puzzle pieces together neatly. Striving for success in your work is a noble intent but cannot serve as your principal aim. You must have a loftier aspiration. If your vocational goals are merely temporal, your head or your heart will succumb to short-term pressures and challenges.

GREAT WORK

Aspiration is an apropos term as we consider the relationship between our work and our lives. I believe that deep down, every person aspires to greatness. While our work does not define us, it is a primary tool our Maker uses to mold and shape us. We ourselves are works in process. We are being formed into some image and advancing toward some mark or standard. Therefore the intersection between our work and our lives is of great importance. Living is a process of becoming, and enjoying our work helps us feel alive.

The late Steve Jobs is recognized as one of the greatest visionaries and innovators in modern history. Jobs founded several innovative companies but is most associated with Apple Inc., the company he led for many years. Products such as the Macintosh Computer, iPod, and iPhone enable the productivity of millions and inspire their creativity as well. By most accounts, Jobs was an intensely driven man who was deeply passionate about his work. Though he passed away, his legacy endures. His work clearly epitomized his passions. His place in eternity is left to our Maker to judge. His testimony in this life taught that meaningful work is one of the greatest rewards life offers.

In 2005, Steve Jobs delivered a deeply personal and deeply moving commencement address at Stanford University.[3] Just one year earlier, he had been diagnosed with a deadly form of pancreatic cancer. He encouraged the newly minted graduates regarding the next chapter of their lives. As they undoubtedly experienced both excitement and apprehension concerning their future, Jobs offered the following admonishment as it pertains to work: "Your work is going to fill a large part of your life, and the only way to be truly satisfied is to do what you believe is great work. And the only way to do great work is to love what you do." The advice of one of the most successful entrepreneurs in modern history was simply to do work that captures your heart. In other words, he encouraged them to discover joy in their work. He went on to remark, "If you haven't found it yet, keep looking. Don't settle. As with all matters of the heart, you'll know when you find it."[4] His advice suggests the discovery of joyful work is related to our choice of occupation.

Useful perspective can be gleaned from Jobs's admonishment. This is especially true if we consider the context. The eager Stanford graduates he addressed undoubtedly had an array of career choices. The broader application of his advice must be tempered by the reality that not everyone is afforded the same opportunities or privilege. Given the choice, I similarly encourage choosing work that aligns with your interests. And while your affinity for your occupation is germane, it is secondary to his principal advice, which is to do great work.

As I reflect on my personal journey, I can also attest that fulfillment comes as a means of a purposeful search. My pursuit, however, is less about finding the right kind of work and more about discovering the joy my present work affords. My aspiration has progressed from doing great work to having a great work life. My encouragement to you is simple. Seek harmony between your personal and professional pursuits, ensuring they intentionally fit together. This will allow the great work you do to become a testimony of a life well lived. To aid you on your journey, here are seven fundamental principles that must be embraced to achieve work-life synergy: (1) work reveals purpose, (2) work requires effort, (3) work promotes growth, (4) work develops skill, (5) work fosters relationships, (6) work produces value, and (7) work glorifies God. The application of these principles, explored in this final section of the book, will enable you to transform your occupation into your vocation. By doing so, you will know the path to discovering joy in your work and fulfillment in your life.

8

WORK REVEALS
PURPOSE

*Everyone has been made for some particular work, and
the desire for that work has been put in every heart.*

RUMI

Nearly two decades ago, my father—who has always been my
foremost mentor, encouraging me toward self-development—
invited me to attend a conference that indelibly influenced my
perspective on work and life. The event was particularly memorable as it took place during Father's Day weekend. I had just
earned my master's degree from the University of Chicago. I was
two weeks removed from my commencement ceremony and two
weeks away from reentering the work force. My time during
graduate school was an important season of introspection and exploration. Attending the full-time MBA program provided me
with the opportunity to thoughtfully reflect on my work experience and career aspiration. While many of my peers were worried
about career advancement, I was concerned about career fulfillment. Something visceral indicated my vocation meant more
than paychecks and promotions. My personal life was also evolving.
My wife had previously obtained her MBA and we were married
just before I started business school. We pondered the important
professional and personal decisions before us.

The keynote conference speaker, the late Dr. Myles Munroe, taught on the topic of potential. I have held tightly to the notes I scribbled from Dr. Munroe's address many years ago. While I didn't write down his words verbatim, he began with an interesting thought exercise. "How do you want to be remembered by family, friends, and coworkers after this life?" He paused for effect. "Most people live their lives without maximizing their potential. Avoid the *tragedy* of taking your potential to the grave!" His message was especially timely for me, given where I was in my professional and personal journey. While he provided many insights, I took away three themes that have influenced my philosophy on work and life. First, we each are personally accountable for unlocking the potential or reserved power inside of us. Second, our life circumstances such as race, culture, or socioeconomic status cannot constrain our potential. Third, our work serves as a principal means of releasing our potential. As Myles emphatically stated, "Work is the master key for releasing potential."

I'd spent the prior two years with some of the most astute and accomplished instructors at the graduate level. Taken together, I had a total of six years of undergraduate and graduate studies focused in the area of business and finance. My advanced studies were specifically intended to prepare me for long-term career success. I had also worked for several years between my undergraduate and graduate school tenures, during which time I had received many formal hours of training. Amid my many hours of instruction, I had never previously been introduced to this concept of potential. Moreover, the idea of work as a transcendent experience was a foreign concept. I knew people who seemed very satisfied with their careers, yet those individuals generally referred to their work as their duty as opposed to their calling. Suddenly, a light bulb went off in my head. Fully unleashing our potential occurs when we connect our work with our purpose. When we commit our hands, head, and heart to our work, work becomes much more than a job. We not only unlock untapped potential, but we also discover many of our deepest passions through our work. This self-discovery helps reveal our reason for living.

LESSONS FROM OUR ELDERS

"Settling into a life of leisure is becoming the exception."[1] A *Bloomberg BusinessWeek* article on retirement caught my attention recently. The article cited research from the National Institute on Aging, which revealed that 40 percent of American workers age sixty-five and older were previously retired. I presumed the article would cite financial hardship as the main reason retirees were returning to the workforce. The article affirmed that an increasing number of retirees are indeed returning to work due to financial necessity. However, the article focused on the broader group of former retirees who have returned to work because they miss the challenge and camaraderie. People commonly assume a life of leisure is the preferred prize for years of hard work. But given the choice, retirees increasingly prefer productive work to leisure activities. This trend is particularly notable among affluent retirees who have sufficient means to support a comfortable lifestyle in retirement.

With age comes insight and wisdom. The old adage rings true: we often don't appreciate what we have until it's gone. What does the experience of our elders teach us about work? Be grateful for the opportunity and ability to work. Work diligently for as long as you are able. And know your work serves a greater, and dare I say, transcendent purpose.

My interactions with two soon-to-be retirees provided me with some fresh insights into the intersection of purpose and work. Interestingly, I learned these lessons on my commute as opposed to in the workplace. Gallup estimates there are nearly 150 million American workers over the age of sixteen, and the overwhelming majority of us commute to work.[2] I live in a suburb and am among the legion of individuals who take commuter rail to my office in the city center. My commute from home to the office is just over an hour, forty-two minutes of which are on the train. People are creatures of habit, so over the years I have traversed back and forth with the same cohort of individuals. In fact, we generally park in the same spots, board through the same doors, and sit in the same seats. I have a relatively long workday and therefore encounter distinct groups of commuters on my morning and evening train rides. Rose was a mainstay on my morning commute, and Eric, a stalwart on my evening commute. It turned out both Rose and Eric were retiring within weeks of one another.

Rose was a gregarious woman who dutifully worked in a clerical capacity for the same employer for many years. While I did not know Rose well, my preferred seat on the commuter train was directly across from hers on our morning commute. Rose was very sociable and wasn't bashful about sharing her opinions on the topic of the day. Whether panning the local sports teams or critiquing the local politicians, Rose provided plenty of color commentary during the morning commute. However, no single topic dominated her conversations more than work. Rose was a dedicated employee who rarely missed a day at the office. Dominant themes in her daily conversations, however, were her interpersonal challenges with her boss and fellow employees. It was clear from her account Rose did not enjoy her work. By her own admission, she felt disconnected from her work and struggled to make it through many days. When she announced her pending retirement, she stated she was literally counting the days until her freedom.

Eric was the polar opposite of Rose. Eric was quiet but had a commanding presence. Though I did not have a personal relationship with Eric, we each preferred the designated quiet car on our evening commute. Eric was a very pleasant gentleman and one day as we disembarked from the train, he offered his typical warm greeting. In our years of commuting together we had never shared more than pleasantries and small talk. He seemed especially cheerful that day, and to my surprise he told me he was retiring from his managerial position with a governmental agency at the end of the year. He proceeded to share details about a retirement party his coworkers held in his honor. Eric was clearly moved as he reflected on the remarks offered by his coworkers. The event concluded with his speech to those who were gathered. He said it was the hardest speech he had ever given. "How do you sum up a career's worth of great experiences and relationships in a few minutes?" he rhetorically asked. It was apparent Eric not only valued his relationship with his coworkers, but he took great pride in his work. After taking an extended vacation, Eric leveraged his professional experience in a new entrepreneurial endeavor serving the local community. Eric is a genuine example of someone who finds joy in his work.

The idea that success and prosperity can be achieved through hard work is a commonly accepted American ideal. The classic American dream was seen as culminating in an extended period of leisure and play. Success was defined as "not working." It is interesting, however, to juxtapose the perspectives of my two fellow commuters. Both had long careers with their respective employers. They nevertheless had very different perspectives on their work experience. Rose was literally counting the days until the end of her tour of duty while Eric was savoring his final days with his present employer. Rose was eager to stop working while Eric was looking forward to a second act during his so-called retirement years. What accounts for the difference? We might easily surmise Eric had a better job or worked for a better employer. However, as I consider their respective testimonies, I believe there is a deeper reason. Rose admitted she was going through the motions and didn't feel a sense of purpose in her work. Eric, conversely, was energized by his work and sought new opportunities. If our work lacks a sense of purpose, it is wearying to the body, mind, and soul.

If we find purpose in our work, the inevitable challenges are a light affliction (2 Cor 4:17).

WORKING THEORY

Work done well aligns us with our purpose for living. Consider how we allocate our time. The typical workday accounts for over 50 percent of our waking hours. This excludes commuting or time dedicated to volunteer work activities. On average, we commit one third of our waking hours to work during our adult lives. From the time we are born, we will commit one out of four of our waking hours to our primary occupation. There is no singular pursuit that demands more of our talent and time. The magnitude of this investment alone demands we examine work's purpose in our lives.

You've heard it said that many people work to live. This implies they toil of necessity to provide the means to support themselves and their families. You've heard it said that other people live to work. The implication is their lives center on their work. Which type of individual are you? Before you answer, consider that these two options are a bit of a false dichotomy. Our practical experience is more often a mix of the two and rarely fully one extreme or the other. Therefore, I'd like to propose a third option. You can choose to come alive through your work. What does it mean to come alive through your work? We are each imbued with power and created for a purpose. The key word here is purpose. You come alive in your work by aligning your work with your purpose.

Theories abound on how work relates to purpose. An entire field of study, in fact, explores the psychology of working. Understanding the role of work in the human experience has been a topic pondered by great minds since early civilization. Rumi, the renowned thirteenth century poet, scholar, and Islamic theologian was one such great mind.[3] The themes expressed in his poetry were considered well ahead of his time. Millions of copies of his poetry are translated and sold posthumously, making him one of the world's most read poets. It is said his writings articulate what it means to be alive. Where do we need to feel alive more than in our daily work? Consider the implications of Rumi's assertion that the desire for work has been put into every heart. This lifelong desire to do meaningful work turns the classic retirement dream on its head. My basis for this truth may differ from Rumi's, but my working theory is analogous. I believe we were especially created for work and we find fulfillment in life when we align our purpose with our work.

How do we align our purpose with our work? That, as they say, is the million-dollar question. While I will not attest to have the ultimate answer, I do have a working theory I test on a daily basis. Much like science experimentation, my current theory is birthed from a failed hypothesis or explanation for the purpose of work. When I first sought to link purpose and work, I initially settled on the view that people were uniquely created for certain work. I still firmly believe there is much to be gained by pursuing an occupation that aligns with your passion and innate skill, but my early under-standing of vocation as a calling primarily entailed identifying the particular work one was created to pursue. Over time I realized my hypothesis was constraining and impractical. It was constraining in that we often obtain the wisdom to make sound vocational choices through trial and error. It was impractical in that there are practical limitations on the vocational choices available to us in the short- and long-term. My hypothesis ultimately failed because the Creator, and not the created being, is the arbiter of the purpose for which we work and live. It's not quite that we are created for certain work, but perhaps more that we are created to work pro-ductively in various contexts and situations. The Creator calls us to exercise our gifts well in whatever occupation we find ourselves at a given time. We are also called be faithful stewards by further developing our talents and bringing them to their full potential through our work. When this becomes your approach, you begin to transform your occupation into your vocation.

For me, the answer to the million-dollar question is an article of both experience and faith. My parents, who are pastors, often remind me of an inspiring passage of Scripture. The apostle Paul, a prolific New Testament writer, implores his readers to have confidence in all circumstances. "And we know that in all things God works for the good of those who love him, who have been called according to his purpose" (Rom 8:28). While there is a very specific context to which he is writing, his words have many applications. My parents taught me that while I might not readily understand every aspect of a situation, I should always act with integrity. My actions in the midst of the situation—as opposed to perfect foreknowledge—are the key to discovering the ultimate meaning and purpose. Moreover, some things I simply can't perceive are working on my behalf.

What does this have to do with work? Instead of trying to find the perfect occupation, focus on being perfected in your daily work. You have innate talent, developed skills, and untapped potential yet to be revealed. While some occupational choices naturally fit you better than others, you can come alive through whatever vocation you are pursuing today. You simply have to give your hands, head, and heart fully to your work. Experience continues to teach me that I can fulfill my life's purpose in any line of work if I allow the Creator to work through me. Your choice of vocation is an important one. A more important choice is to let your Creator work through you.

WORKING THROUGH YOU

We know work is essential to life. Beyond providing sustenance, our work helps give meaning to our life's journey. This is why it is vitally important to align our work with our purpose. How do we practically accomplish this? It requires we work in such a way that indicates the existence of a purpose. Said another way, our actions must be purposeful. Purposeful work isn't defined by the nature of the task. Recall Dr. King's encouragement to the would-be street sweeper. He affirms there is dignity, value, and purpose in every type of work. We innately desire to do meaningful work. This is self-evident to most people. A related truth is less evident to many people: we have the ability to give our work meaning. We give our work meaning by being purposeful. Being purposeful means to be fully determined to release your potential through your work. No matter the task, big or small, endeavor to give it your all. It is by demonstrating this quality of purposefulness we discover aspects of our calling or purpose.

My wife and I have been blessed to have purposeful people in our lives who serve as sources of inspiration. One particular bright light is Sharon. Sharon is a hairstylist by profession, but to her clients she is so much more. Sharon has been my wife's personal stylist for twenty-two years. Beyond being exceptionally skilled at her craft, she uses her many gifts to brighten the lives of the people she serves. Sharon selected cosmetology as a major in high school. She worked as an assistant in a salon while in high school to earn extra money. After getting her cosmetology license, she continued to work as a stylist to pay for higher education.

One day I asked Sharon why she chose her occupation. "Initially I was focused on the money that I could make to pay for college. I was determined to get my degree, which motivated me to work hard as a stylist." Upon earning her degree, Sharon realized that not only was she a talented stylist but also, she had a knack for business. Sharon became a business owner, opening her own salon. Sharon employs and trains young women, leads an organization that mentors young women, and serves as a writer and editor for a magazine. And yes, she continues her primary occupation as a hairstylist. Sharon loves her work and is loved by her clients. "The thing that gives me the most joy is seeing someone's face light up after I give them a new hairstyle. If I can help them feel better by enhancing their look, then I have done my job well," says Sharon. She understands that her occupation provides a platform to positively impact people's lives. Sharon is very dear to us, and we have enjoyed watching her flourish in her vocational pursuits. The purposefulness with which she pursues her work helps others more clearly see their beauty, both inside and out.

A sound philosophy toward work helps reveal three truths. First, your choice of vocation does not define you. Your profession depicts what you currently do as opposed to what you have the potential to become. Your approach to your work does, however, shape you. Purposeful work is an important means by which the Creator perfects you. Who you are—and who you are becoming—is revealed through your work. Second, your choice of vocation does not determine your value. Your contribution in life is measured by what you do with the time, talent, and opportunities you have been afforded. Your compensation doesn't count when it comes to maximizing your potential and fulfilling your purpose. You create lasting value by doing purposeful work. Third, and most important, your choice of vocation does not define your purpose. It is more of a means to a greater end. You discover your calling or purpose by doing purposeful work.

Let me encourage you with a final affirmation. You are here on purpose. Wherever *here* is, you are *here* on purpose. Your life is the result of a deliberate choice by your Creator. This also means your life and your work have a purpose. The unique circumstances of your birth conceal the reason for your existence. This is why work is a God-given gift. The ability to employ your mind, body, and soul through your work reveals your purpose. In this regard, I agree with Rumi's contention that every human being has been made for some work. The desire to work is linked to the desire to fulfill your purpose. You are not, however, destined for a specific vocation or type of work. You and I have the capacity to demonstrate purposefulness in any type of work we choose. When we tap into this capacity, we feel as though we lose ourselves in our work.

This is what a renowned psychologist called "flow," advanced in his bestselling book by the same title. Flow is described as a state of consciousness where people experience deep enjoyment, creativity, and engagement.[4] For me, this can occur in a professional setting or in volunteering at a local charity. It can occur while writing a manuscript or cleaning the garage on the weekend. Something truly special happens to us on these occasions. We are free from worry, envy, and self-centeredness. We feel in sync with all of creation. We feel the Creator working in us and through us. We feel a spiritual alignment with our purpose. And we feel utter and complete joy in our work.

CHAPTER 8 REFLECTIONS

Work Reveals Purpose

KEY INSIGHTS

- Discovering your potential connects your work with your purpose.

- Commit your hands, head, and heart to your work to unleash your full potential.

- Work without purpose is wearying to the body, mind, and soul. Find purpose in your work and the inevitable challenges are a light affliction.

- Appreciate the opportunity and ability to work. Work diligently and know that your work serves a greater, transcendent purpose.

- Allow your daily work to perfect you instead of searching for the perfect occupation.

- Your choice of vocation does not define you. However, your approach to your work helps to shape and mold you.

- You are not destined for a specific vocation or type of work. You have the capacity to demonstrate purposefulness in any type of work you choose.

9

WORK REQUIRES EFFORT

Nothing ever comes to one, that is worth
having, except as a result of hard work.

By nature and nurture, I have an affinity for hard work. It partly reflects my achievement leaning. I derive genuine satisfaction from the completion of a challenging task and a job well done. My father was, and is, my role model in this regard. He was a stationary engineer by trade and a skilled handyman by necessity. My siblings and I would joke that nothing was ever truly broken in our home. Dad either knew how to fix it or he would figure it out. No instructions were required. In practice, I have never been as facile with my hands as my father. His example did, however, help impress on me a deep appreciation for hard work and hands-on experience. In my vocational responsibilities, I like to figuratively roll up my sleeves and participate in the various aspects of our work. A mentor who shared similar qualities with my father said that no matter how high you rise in the hierarchy, it is always important to engage in real work. This holds true for my avocational activities as well. Around the house, I enjoy hands-on activities such as yard work or snow removal. Some will argue these tasks are time consuming and more readily outsourced. While there is undoubtedly truth to that perspective, I have learned valuable lessons by simply committing to hands-on work.

One such example occurred last summer. I awoke to a rare Saturday when the calendar was not filled with preexisting commitments. My incomplete punch list included power washing the deck, and there seemed to be no better time than the present. I was also itching to try out the new power washer I had purchased a couple months prior. (Yes, even adults have toys.) To do the job right, I would need to pretreat and manually scrub the deck. Following this step, I could proceed with power washing the deck, which was a tedious task. I estimated the whole endeavor would take about three hours. I elicited the assistance of my sons. The objective was not so much to reduce the workload, and in practice their lack of experience and need for instruction time slowed down the process. However, this task created an opportunity for father-son bonding as well as the opportunity to demonstrate the value of hard work. They were willing subjects, albeit not particularly practiced in the chosen line of work. The promise of ultimately getting to handle the power washer proved to be a helpful enticement. It also proved wise not to mention how long I expected the task to take. Youthfulness and ignorance are bliss.

The first hour was the most challenging. We treated the deck with a detergent solution and manually scrubbed the deck with a brush. Loosening the buildup that had accumulated in the off-season required good-old fashioned elbow grease. Rather than rush through the process, we took turns scrubbing the deck. I demonstrated to them the proper technique and assured the task was done thoroughly. Next we enlisted the power washer. Although we were machine-enabled, this stage took twice as long. I had learned from prior experience the approach required was methodical and patient to cover the intricate areas of the deck and gazebo. Like the first stage, we took turns operating the power washer. About halfway through this stage, my visiting mother-in-law joined us on the deck. After observing us for a while, she asked me if she could give the power washer a whirl. She is a pillar of good health and seemed quite intent, so I handed over the controls. What happened next was unexpected but instructive. She proceeded to work effortlessly with the power washer cleaning portions of the deck. She even refused my first overture to relieve her from the work. While my sons were willing workers, she went about the task gleefully. I initially felt awkward because I felt she should be relaxing. She's certainly earned the right. However, I thought better and let her carry on, as it was plain to see she was enjoying herself.

DIGGING DEEP

Our parents never really stop teaching and mentoring us. Here again my mother-in-law was teaching us valuable lessons through her example. She is rightly qualified to teach most people a thing or two about hard work. During her midlife, my mother-in-law moved to the state of Florida, a preferred retirement destination (among other qualities). Although she is a prodigious saver, she worked well into her seventies. She was never in a hurry to retire and, though she is now technically retired, Mom is as busy as ever. She has picked up a part-time job and volunteers weekly for several charitable causes. Mom doesn't work out of necessity as my in-laws are financially savvy and secure. Hard work doesn't just apply to her vocation but her avocation as well. When mom visits, she hardly comports herself as a guest. She is always pitching in and helping. This, of course, is hardly surprising to me because my lovely wife has always modeled the same qualities. The frugality my wife inherited from her mom is matched by a tireless work ethic. I met my wife when she was a full-time student working part time to help pay her way through college. She completed her undergraduate degree in three and a half years while many peers customarily took four to five years. Whether in their professional or personal lives, I've never seen these women I admire shy away from hard work. As they say, the acorn doesn't fall far from the tree.

I have observed that people who work hard are disciplined and focused. Desired outcomes aren't achieved by happenstance but are instead achieved on purpose. I have also observed hard work entails more than just earnestness of effort and should not be confused with aimless striving. My living examples have also revealed several simple truths through their approach. The first and most abiding truth is that meaningful work requires extensive effort. Both the output and effort we extend are a blessing to others and us. The second truth is hard work can—and in fact, should—be enjoyable. My most challenging tasks often produce my deepest sense of fulfillment. The third truth speaks to the quality of our effort. Work requires more than just able bodies and helping hands. Equally important is the type of effort we demonstrate. Specifically, we must be dedicated, enthusiastic, experienced, and persistent. The combination of these qualities enables hard work and together they produce exceptional results. A simple acronym for remembering this concept is this: hard work requires you to dig DEEP. Consistently demonstrating the qualities of *dedication, enthusiasm, experience*, and *persistence* will ensure you are highly productive, and you ultimately find joy in even the most challenging work. Let's dig deeper into these four qualities.

ARE YOU FULLY DEDICATED?

Dedication is the first quality. Dedication reflects our level of commitment to a task or mission. Dedication is evidenced in part by the time and effort we devote to our work. While dedication is a time-tested quality, it isn't simply a function of time served. It is more aptly reflected by the quality of our engagement with our work. Dedicated workers regularly make sacrifices to achieve their vocational goals. This attitude of the mind is cultivated through personal discipline. This is an important insight because through our daily disciplines, we nurture the quality of dedication. Delivering results requires a sustained and, at times, arduous effort. Our most demanding assignments often give us the greatest fulfillment. One of my early mentors would often remind me that hard work builds character. It also helps foster the quality of dedication if we maintain a healthy attitude. This is not to imply hard work is synonymous with dedication. It is better stated thus: the quality of dedication causes us to embrace hard work and sustain the necessary effort to accomplish our objectives.

An exploration of the quality of dedication evokes questions from workers young and old. Is it an innate quality or can it be developed? How do you maintain a high level of commitment over the course of your career? To what or whom are you committed? As I have personally considered these issues, I have come to at least one conclusion. To truly dedicate ourselves, we must first address our natural tendency toward selfishness.

The common perception of a dedicated worker is an individual who compulsively works long and hard hours, the suggestion being that this conduct demonstrates the person's level of commitment. But this turns out to be a counterfeit form of dedication because it is a selfish approach rather than a selfless approach. We might commonly refer to this type of individual as a workaholic. While the effort may be respectable, the motivation often is not pure. The primary motivations of the workaholic are often money, power, or recognition. It is unquestionably true that these things can be obtained through hard work. It is not true, however, that workaholism reflects dedication or selflessness. We all have personal goals related to our work. However, the truly dedicated worker is committed to achieving the shared mission and honoring their commitments to those they serve. It is only when we sacrifice for the benefit of our coworkers and the fulfillment of the mission that we are truly dedicated to our work.

DON'T CURB YOUR ENTHUSIASM!

Enthusiasm is the second quality. Enthusiasm is an active or lively interest in something one enjoys or is passionate about. Enthusiasm is an attitude of the heart, evidenced by the zeal we display and the related emotions it evokes from others. Enthusiasm is a quality perceived with our emotional intelligence. What does enthusiasm look like in practice? The first thing we generally observe about enthusiastic people is the way they describe their work. They speak positively about their work and their coworkers and come across as people who enjoy what they do. Enthusiasm is generally demonstrated in the level of their effort. Enthusiastic workers will often go beyond what is required for a particular task. They generally do so with a smile, reflecting an upbeat attitude. Finally, enthusiastic workers willingly help coworkers to ensure the job is done well. Enthusiastic individuals emit positive emotional energy others can feel. This positively affects coworkers, contributing to a productive work environment.

We instinctively recognize this quality in others but may find it more challenging to cultivate within ourselves. This is partly due to our tendency to look toward external stimuli for motivation for our work. Enthusiasm, like all attitudes of the heart, emanates from the inside. This holds true for our personal and professional pursuits. It is not just important but vital we do not let temporary circumstances or setbacks curb our enthusiasm for our work.

The quality of enthusiasm is the product of two traits. The first trait relates to self-knowledge and clearly established personal values. Your values reflect your deeply held personal beliefs. They signify what is important to you as opposed to what is pleasing to others. A clear set of personal values provides the basis for having the proper attitude toward your work. The lively interest characterized by enthusiasm is most readily developed when you clearly know your personal values. This also extends to aligning your values with your vocation because you achieve more when you are engaged in work you are passionate about. The second trait that promotes enthusiasm is the ability to make wise choices with respect to your vocation and your workplace. Making wise vocational choices has less to do with your preferences and more to do with your productivity. When you choose a vocation that readily allows you to deploy your talents, you have a clear sense of purpose. Similarly, when you choose a workplace where your personal values align with the organizational culture, you have a clear sense of belonging. When you have confidence in your convictions and your contributions, you enthusiastically commit your time and talent to your work.

GET REAL EXPERIENCE

Experience is the third quality. Experience refers to knowledge or skill acquired though application. Experience is evidenced by the level of mastery we have with respect to our vocation. Experience applies to what we do and how we do it. For example, my financial acumen has grown considerably given my years of experience within financial services. The experience I have acquired enables me to provide subject matter expertise to the stakeholders I serve. My cumulative experience also influences how I approach my daily work. The quality of my decision-making has improved because of the experience I have gained.

While experience is a time-tested quality, it is not merely a function of years of service. Similarly, age is not a proxy for the quality of our work experience. In practice, I have found workers may vary significantly in age but have comparable levels of expertise. Experience, then, is a function of our habits. Will Durant, an American writer and philosopher, captured this sentiment aptly when he penned, "We are what we repeatedly do. Excellence, then, is not an act, but a habit."[1] The same can be said of experience.

Intuitively, we recognize the value of professional experience. Consider the questions we ask when we hire a service provider.

"How long have you been in business? How many customers have you served? Will you provide references?" What's the common link? Each of these inquiries relate to the provider's level of experience. And it works the same way when the shoe is on the other foot. Consider the jobs you've applied for in the past. What did the prospective employers inquire about? The interviews invariably revolved around your work experience. The rationale is simple. When it comes to producing quality work, relevant experience matters. So how do we develop this quality? If I were to sum it up in one word, it would be *practice*. While practice doesn't make you perfect, it does perfect you. This is unquestionably true as it applies to your vocation. The most practiced professionals are the most experienced. I have also observed the most practiced professionals are active learners. You must continually attain knowledge and competencies relevant to your vocation. You must identify wise mentors and learn from their experience. Finally, you must apply your increased aptitude every chance you get. This is how you gain experience and, in the process, make valuable contributions through your work.

THE PERSISTENT PREVAIL

Persistence is the fourth and final quality. Persistence is focused determination. It is common to experience difficult seasons during our careers. More practically, we face both expected and unanticipated workplace challenges daily. Some degree of adversity is virtually inevitable. Persistence is evidenced by the resolve to continue despite difficulty, opposition, or failure. Since work involves achieving targeted outcomes amid unpredictable circumstances, persistence is an essential quality. And while persistence is an essential quality, it is not commonly observed. Though intellect and talent abound in the professional arena, many individuals lack the patient endurance required to achieve meaningful objectives. Patience is an increasingly rare virtue. A wise man once presciently observed that patience enables a perfecting process (Jas 1:4)—the implication being both the product of our work as well as our character is perfected if we are willing to persevere.

My sister effectively models the quality of persistence. The youngest of four siblings and the only female in the bunch, she has many unique qualities. It is in many ways fitting that her friends call her Star. Among Star's many qualities is the character trait of "true grit." As her older brother, I've had the vantage point of watching her flourish over time. Star went away for college with aspirations of pursuing a career in business but left school after her first year. After returning home for a short while, she moved away to another state for a fresh start. Star ultimately worked her way into a successful sales role, married, and started a family. Star, however, wasn't satisfied. Among other goals, she wanted to obtain her degree and set an example for her two young daughters. In the midst of raising a young family, she decided she would return to school and complete her degree in business administration. She had unwavering support from her husband and her family. In true Star fashion, she didn't just matriculate through the program but graduated with honors. In fact, she completed the program with a perfect 4.0 grade point average. Today, she works as a manager at a private staffing firm whose mission is to match talented individuals with positions in professional fields and skilled trades. She does this all while passing on her character traits and values to her children.

Persistence is an acquired trait, a quality that can be developed. While our circumstances may foster this virtue, persistence is not a quality we are born with. I believe the key to developing the quality of persistence lies in the definition I offered above. Patience requires focus. More specifically, it requires an intentional focus on the outcome or goal. In many respects, the quality of persistence cultivates the other qualities. You must focus on your goal regardless of what you encounter along the way. This was certainly true for my sister, who didn't let temporary circumstances distract her from her long-term goals. If we revisit our running metaphor, other runners or the conditions of the course can't distract you. You are rightly running your own race.

Similarly, your work requires an intentional focus. You must organize your energy and effort around achieving the shared mission or goal. This kind of focus extends beyond the immediate task at hand. This kind of focus also requires you to ignore distractions and endure disappointment. Maintaining the proper mental focus enables your persistence and ensures your performance. In work and in life, those who are persistent ultimately prevail.

IT'S WORTH THE WORK

Genuine work always produces valuable output. We might think of this as a proverbial harvest. We must recognize the commensurate cost required to reap this reward—in most instances, tried-and-true hard work. The value produced relates directly to the quality of the effort given. Booker T. Washington, the respected educator, author, and statesman, certainly knew a thing or two about hard work. Born into slavery in 1856, he first experienced freedom at nine years of age following the abolishment of slavery in America. A young Booker taught himself to read prior to attending primary school. He would later work in salt furnaces and coal mines to pursue his goal of obtaining higher education. He pressed on, working his way through college and receiving degrees from Hampton University and Virginia Union. While he is known to many for his pioneering leadership of Tuskegee Institution, authorship of fourteen books, and advisory role to US Presidents Theodore Roosevelt and William Taft, his life's work is epitomized by the quality of persistence and the way he embraced hard work.

In the preceding passages, I've shared firsthand accounts from the lives of my parents, in-laws, wife, sister, and mentors. Each of these individuals has directly modeled hard work for me. Booker

T. Washington is a historical figure who has served as a role model to many in this regard. As it pertains to their vocation and their life's work, they all seem to share certain traits that drove them. Prevalent among these are the qualities of dedication, enthusiasm, experience and persistence; they were all willing to dig DEEP to do meaningful work. Our work experience is ultimately what we decide to make of it. We can be highly productive and be perfected in the process if we are willing subjects. I admonish you to dig DEEP, knowing that if you are dedicated, enthusiastic, experienced, and persistent, you will undoubtedly produce great workmanship. More important, your effort will lead to the discovery of true joy in your work.

Work Requires Effort

——

KEY INSIGHTS

- Work challenges you physically, mentally, and spiritually, and results are achieved on purpose.

- Hard work is enjoyable; your most challenging tasks produce a deep sense of fulfillment.

- Work requires you to dig DEEP: be dedicated, enthusiastic, experienced, and persistent.

- Commit to serve others and honor your commitments.

- Do not let temporary circumstances or setbacks curb your enthusiasm.

- While practice does not make you perfect, patience will perfect you.

- Persistence in the face of challenges paves the path to fulfillment.

WORK PROMOTES GROWTH

*Big jobs usually go to individuals who prove
their ability to outgrow small ones.*

RALPH WALDO EMERSON

About nine years ago, a colleague directed a young professional to seek me out for career advice. Maria had joined the company soon after completing her undergraduate degree. She was early into her career experience, having worked for the company for three years. She dutifully contacted me to arrange a meeting. I agreed to meet with her subject to a routine request. I asked her to articulate her objectives for the meeting. I recall her response largely because of her forthrightness. Maria had networked with several senior professionals but had never been asked to convey her objectives in advance. My question caused her to critically examine her intent for the meeting. Her prior dialogues with senior professionals had followed a recurrent line of questioning: How did you advance to your current position? To what do you attribute your success? How can I achieve similar success? After reflecting on my request, she posed only one question in her email. What would I ask, if I were in her shoes? People frequently ask me for career advice, and in most cases their meaning boils down to how they can advance their career. I offered a more valuable exploration, which involved professional and personal growth.

We began our first meeting with a friendly exchange about our respective backgrounds and interests. Maria was intellectually curious and detail-oriented. Though a natural introvert, she was very sociable. Her disarming persona veiled a strong ambition. She was acutely focused on her career progression. "What are your foremost personal values?" I asked.

"I'm not sure I understand what you mean," she remarked.

"Values are deeply held beliefs that affect every area of our lives. Having a clear sense of personal values is essential to navigating your career. I can provide you with more appropriate career guidance if I understand what's truly important to you."

"My faith and my family are the most important things in my life," she replied. This revelation proved to be an inflection point in our dialogue as we shared similar personal priorities. This also began an informal mentoring relationship that would persist for several years. Maria focused on aligning her career ambitions with her personal priorities.

Our most important career choices are generally values-based decisions. This includes decisions such as which organization offers the best cultural fit and what type of position to pursue. My personal values include faith, relationships, wisdom, accountability, leadership, competence, and generosity. Understanding your values helps align your career aspirations with your greater purpose. Wise career advice entails more than tactics for career advancement. And your vocation offers you much more than means to your desired ends. Work promotes growth. Specifically, it cultivates professional development and personal maturity. We will explore both the professional and personal aspects of growth to better understand how they relate to our work.

PROFESSIONAL DEVELOPMENT

Have you ever heard someone referred to as a "consummate professional"? *Consummate* means extremely skilled or accomplished. In a word, it means *complete*. A consummate professional is highly effective at applying what he or she knows. Consummate professionals do not merit this distinction simply because they are talented. We are each imbued with God-given talents, so our giftedness alone does not make us consummate professionals. The only way to maximize our impact is to maximize and improve upon our talent. In chapter three, I outlined three dimensions of aptitude: *discovery*, *development*, and *deployment*. Development involves honing your talents and is synonymous with growth. Three forms of learning principally drive professional development: (1) instruction, (2) association, and (3) application. We will explore how each of these facets of professional development promotes growth and fulfillment.

Instruction. My family has a history of military service, including my father, who proudly served in the United States Air Force. One of the principal benefits those who served highlight is the rigorous and valuable training they received. Initial military training is generally divided into two segments. Basic training, or boot camp, entails physical, mental, and emotional preparation to ensure recruits are combat-ready. This common training program provides service members with the basic tools necessary to perform their roles during their tours of duty. After basic training, which lasts for about three to four months, service members receive advanced individual training based on their chosen vocational field. This segment of training equips service members with competencies that can be deployed during their service within the military and beyond. This period of training lasts from one to twelve months depending on the area of specialty. The objective of military training is to ensure recruits are capable and confident. The military provides ongoing professional development by continually training and testing service members in the areas of fitness, combat readiness, and occupational proficiency.

The military offers a poignant example of the first aspect of professional development, which is learning through instruction. Training involves instruction in a skill or competency. Basic competencies are required for all vocations. Consummate professionals are distinguished by their commitment to expanding their knowledge and proficiency through instruction. They don't simply complete basic training but rather seek to become expert practitioners. High performing enterprises spend more than their competitors on training. Similarly, the highest performing workers avail themselves of formal and informal instruction. Instruction may be received through the attainment of professional degrees or certifications. Instruction may also take the form of professional programs, workshops, or seminars. Taken together these varied forms of instruction provide the means to enhance your existing competencies and learn new ones. You must invest time and money to reap the benefits of instruction. This investment, however, yields exponential returns. Learning through instruction is an elemental facet of your professional development and lays the foundation for all other aspects.

Association. Learning through association is the second aspect of professional development. In this context, *association* refers to a connection or relationship. Cultivating a network of professional relationships is essential to your professional growth. Relationships allow you to benefit from the knowledge, experience, and affiliations of other professionals. Relationships with subject matter experts allow you to expand your knowledge base. Relationships with advisers help you solve problems and make wise decisions. Relationships with trusted colleagues provide timely feedback, which allows you to improve your effectiveness working with others. Mentors and sponsors are particularly integral to our professional development. Mentors are living examples who provide guidance and support. Sponsors are influential persons who advocate for you. Taken together, these represent a cadre of valuable relationships that help you prosper professionally. Whether our associations are formal or informal, we flourish if we have role models who show us the way.

The term *role model* describes a person whose behaviors, qualities, and achievements serve as an example for others. Individuals often compare themselves to people who occupy a position to which they aspire. This is common with respect to occupational pursuits and is a construct that has existed over time. Historically, it was common to pursue an occupation or trade through an apprenticeship. An experienced professional provided instruction and modeled the actions and personal attributes the novice needed to become successful. The relationship was essential for professional success. While formal apprenticeships are less common today, our professional relationships serve a vital role in our professional development. Ethan, an emergency room doctor, is a good friend. He has a warm personality and chose the medical profession to help people live better lives. Ethan described himself as an average student who was unsure of his career path during his early college years. That was until he met a physician who began to mentor him. His mentor not only introduced Ethan to the field of medicine but also provided him with other contacts in the medical field. These associations provided recommendations for medical school, encouragement during his matriculation, and guidance during his medical internship. Ethan says these associations were essential for his development as a physician. He now pays their investment forward by mentoring young physicians and helping disadvantaged youths pursue careers in medicine.

Application. During my career, I have pursued several entrepreneurial endeavors ranging from starting a small business to launching a new business unit as part of a large organization. I naturally have a strong affinity and respect for entrepreneurs and have studied many examples. An entrepreneur is someone who exercises initiative and takes the risk to pursue a business opportunity. While we recognize some entrepreneurs as highly innovative and others as visionary, most possess a basic quality indispensable for all workers: entrepreneurs are highly adept at active learning. While others study the problem or opportunity, individuals with an entrepreneurial spirit just do it. They tap into the lifeblood of ingenuity that runs through humankind and apply their hands, head, and heart to doing real work. The very nature of tackling new things requires a degree of trial and error. In this way, they learn from their successes and their failures. They not only increase their productivity but also develop skills such as planning, managing, and leading in the process. The discipline of learning by doing provides them with plenty of practice and actionable feedback.

Learning through application is the third and most hands-on aspect of professional development. Work involves specific duties or responsibilities. While certain aspects of our work are learned through instruction and others are learned though association, application is where the rubber meets the road. Each workday presents us with opportunities to produce valuable outputs while learning in the process. When we earnestly apply ourselves to our work assignments, we increase our aptitude. This applied learning perfects our mastery of the specific competencies required to perform our role and our ability to interact harmoniously with other people. Professional challenges test our aptitude and cause us to effectively apply what we have learned. The willingness to assume additional duties or responsibilities provides us with fresh developmental opportunities. Again, provide more service than your pay dictates. This type of work ethic establishes effective work habits. Like entrepreneurs, consummate professionals are adept at learning and growing through application.

THE MARKS OF MATURITY

While professional growth is our foundational focus, work affords equally valuable opportunities to grow personally. Personal maturity is about increasing our self-awareness and establishing our unique identity. This type of character formation, which differs from professional development, is more aptly defined as personal maturity. We exhibit personal maturity by our ability to respond to changes in our environment constructively and appropriately. While professional development is linked to our aptitude, personal maturity is principally a function of our attitude. The marks of maturity are tangible. Intentionality, the ability to focus amid potential distractions, is one example. The ability to delay gratification and prioritize the needs of others is another. The ability to follow through on commitments even when the task is no longer new or novel is also an important trait. Finally, the ability to absorb both praise and criticism in a balanced manner is a clear sign of maturity. Personal maturity embraces four facets of our conscious and unconscious experience, shaping us intellectually, emotionally, socially and spiritually. We will explore how each of these facets of personal maturity promotes growth and fulfillment.

Intellectual maturity, the first element of personal maturity, relates to our ability to think and learn. We are intellectual beings. Work affords us opportunities to develop our intelligence and also allows us to develop critical thinking skills. While intellectual maturity reflects our cognitive skills, such as the ability to learn and retain knowledge, there are other essential aspects of intellectual maturity. A fundamental aspect is the ability to solve problems. From an early age, we learn the basic framework of problem solving: determining who, what, when, where, why, and how. With application, our critical thinking capacity develops. This allows us to solve more complex problems and helps us deal with increased uncertainty.

Intellectual maturity increases our intellectual curiosity, creating a thirst for knowledge as well as the ability to find value in differing perspectives. The greatest sign of intellectual maturity is the understanding that you are always, ever learning. This produces an attitude that keeps you open to new ways of learning.

Emotional maturity is the second element of personal maturity and relates to our ability to manage our feelings. We are emotional beings. In fact, the emotional parts of our brain known as our limbic system respond to external stimuli far more quickly than the cognitive parts of our brain. Emotions are linked to memories and experiences and are not consciously controlled.

If we seek to better manage our emotions, much of the work must be done in advance of the circumstances that demand it. For example, we must first be aware of the importance of tending to our emotional well-being. Rather than suppress bad experiences, we should seek counsel and guidance. Emotions should never be bottled up, but rather we must find healthy outlets. We should actively create positive experiences and engagement with our work and coworkers. This creates a reservoir of positive emotional energy to draw from. Finally, we must condition ourselves not to react immediately. The first thoughts that come rushing to your mind are generally dominated by your feelings. Emotional maturity is knowing your emotions count, but they must not count too much. Emotional maturity leads you to a higher level of self-awareness. It also encourages patience, which contributes to the perfecting work of helping you mature.

Social maturity is the third element of personal maturity and relates to our ability to relate to others. We are social beings who live and work in community. Social maturity is the natural successor to emotional maturity because it largely involves developing empathy for others. Seeking to understand the feelings and experiences of others is a foundational element of social maturity. The most telling sign of immaturity is selfishness. Our social interactions at work present us with the opportunity to become more selfless.

Work by its very nature develops our capacity to constructively engage with others. In dealing with the inevitable pressures and conflicts in the workplace, we develop our interpersonal skills. Collaboration requires us to become more objective and less subjective because we must incorporate the experiences and perspectives of others. Moreover, we build on our emotional maturity through compassionate engagement with others, learning valuable lessons in self-control and cultural awareness. Social maturity affords you a higher level of cultural awareness and reveals accepted norms and behaviors. More importantly, social maturity enables you to develop healthy working relationships with your coworkers, leading to greater personal growth and fulfillment. You grow by means of your social connections.

Spiritual maturity is the fourth and final element of personal maturity and relates to our ability to develop our inner lives. We are living souls, and we have a spiritual existence. Our faith orientation often informs our spiritual maturity. My faith plays an essential role in my personal development, including shaping my views toward my work. The most universal link between work and spiritual maturity is our inherent need to find meaningfulness in our work. A clear sign of spiritual maturity is both the search for and attainment of fulfillment in our work. Our ability to find a calling or purpose in our work ventures beyond our career search and intersects with our spiritual journey.

Spiritual maturity is often evidenced by a strong desire to seek and apply truth. Life is less about seeking what is pleasurable but rather seeking what is just or right. Spiritual maturity is marked by a distinct focus on the soul. Your work experience literally helps to shape your inner self. Spiritually mature individuals spend less time managing perceptions and pleasing others. Your contentment comes from knowing you are valued by your Creator and not by what you create. Spiritual maturity ultimately changes the way you view your vocation. Your work is part of a greater purpose and a higher calling to serve humanity.

GROWING PAYS

I recently had an unexpected visit from Maria. Several years prior, she accepted a position in a new geographic market. I had not seen or spoken with her in the ensuing five years. Her visit was a welcome surprise. Quite a bit had transpired since our last meeting. Professionally, she was on the fast track at the company. She had received two promotions following her move. Moreover, she had assumed a range of functional responsibilities and was now a manager leading a team of eleven coworkers. She displayed a quiet confidence that corresponded with her growing professional experience. Her personal situation had also evolved. She now had two young children and reveled in her time with her growing family. I recounted from our past dialogues that she deeply valued quality time with family. This season of life naturally brought opportunities and challenges as she and her spouse balanced budding careers and growing family commitments. I wasn't surprised one bit by her career advancement. I was, however, interested in hearing more about her professional and personal journey.

Maria described the intervening years since we last connected as a demanding yet rewarding period. Neither she nor her spouse had close family or friends in the market where they relocated. The challenge of establishing new relationships while taking on a stretch assignment was initially a daunting task. Her positive attitude allowed her to flourish amid those circumstances. The birth of their first child introduced a new set of challenges. Clarity with respect to her personal values allowed her to navigate the associated trials. I was pleased to learn our conversations had proved helpful during those periods. She was now contemplating a business development role to deepen her sales and client relationship experience. She surmised increasing that skill set would position her to become a managing executive of a regional market. "Do you have any advice for me regarding the new managing executive role?" Maria asked. I could tell she was anxious about the decision.

"What are your long-term career objectives?" I replied.

"I'd like to join the company's executive management group. Some people may view it as a stretch, but I can see myself in that type of position." This was no small ambition. I certainly couldn't guarantee she would land in the C-suite. I did, however, assure her she would continue to grow professionally and personally by maintaining the proper focus. I promised to continue to provide counsel and encouragement along the way. Who knows? The combination of discipline, mentorship, and grace just might land her one of those executive roles one day.

Our conversations from the past focused on professional and personal growth. She had advanced quickly in her career and now had her sights set on a "big" job. Just as before, she would figuratively have to grow into her desired position. She possessed the aptitude and determination. The enabler in the long run would be the proper attitude. The lesson is clear. Committing to professional and personal growth positions you for future promotion. Growth does not guarantee you will get the job of your dreams. It does, however, prepare you for whatever big roles come your way. Professional development is the first facet of growth. This is accomplished through three forms of learning, which include instruction, association, and application. You must add personal maturity, which is the second facet of growth. You must grow intellectually, emotionally, socially, and spiritually. Taking individual accountability for your professional development and personal maturity will take your career to heights your ambition never will. Goals are important for achieving your career aspirations. Growth is, however, essential to experiencing joy in your work.

CHAPTER 10 REFLECTIONS

Work Promotes Growth

KEY INSIGHTS

- Pursue professional growth through employee training, advanced degrees, certification programs, workshops, or seminars.

- Cultivate professional relationships in order to grow from the knowledge, experience, perspective, and affiliations of others.

- Firsthand experience and timely feedback are key contributors to your professional growth.

- Personal maturity entails growing intellectually, emotionally, socially, and spiritually.

- Curiosity and open-mindedness are signs of intellectual maturity.

- Compassionate engagement with others leads to greater self-awareness and self-control.

- Spiritual maturity is evidenced by a deep desire to find meaning in work. The pursuit of professional and personal growth aligns your work with your greater purpose.

WORK DEVELOPS SKILL

What you are will show in what you do.

Thomas Davidson

A résumé is commonly required for most professional pursuits, so I trust you've written one or more. Whether considering external or internal candidates, the recruitment process generally begins with reviewing résumés. While your résumé may be utilized to assess your qualifications for a position, it is intended to capture much more than your work history. The purpose is to provide a summary of your qualifications, accomplishments, and abilities. It is not necessarily a tool for seeking employment opportunities away from your current employer. In fact, résumés are frequently utilized to explore new career opportunities with a current employer. Submitting one is also a common requirement for nonprofit service, professional development opportunities, and post-secondary educational programs. If composed well, your résumé provides reviewers with insight into your innate abilities and acquired competencies. For me, a lesson on effective résumé writing revealed a more profound truth regarding skill development through our work.

In addition to working in the corporate sector, I've pursued several entrepreneurial endeavors. One such endeavor was a business partnership with a friend. We were employees by day and entrepreneurs by night. We were also long on ideas and short on capital. It turns out our ideas held the key to attracting more capital, but it required some introspection. We entered a business case challenge that offered grants to the winning presenters. Applicants were required to submit a detailed business plan as well as résumés for the first round of the competition. As we assembled our materials for submission, I noticed ours were demonstrably different. I provided a concise summary of my educational background and a chronological listing of my work experience. I concluded with a one-liner that cited a few personal interests—a standard format. My partner, by contrast, began his with a personalized statement about his unique abilities. The section on his professional experience enumerated his responsibilities and articulated measurable outcomes achieved. He also identified specific competencies he acquired. He concluded with a thoughtful summary of his outside interests that aligned with his overall profile. Our résumés weren't simply demonstrably different. His was demonstrably better.

When I inquired about it, he noted he'd recently done a makeover of his résumé inspired by an article on effective résumé writing. In short, he stated he wanted his to better reflect his distinctiveness. While I fancied the revised format and thoughtful composition of it, his response really got my attention. It occurred to me my résumé had the potential to have greater impact than I'd previously thought as its purpose is neither to summarize experience and credentials nor solely to attract employment or business opportunities. His example demonstrated that a résumé should provide insight about one's unique skillset. A skillset is what potential employers, customers, investors, and other stakeholders are keenly interested in. There is, of course, a catch. You must have a deep understanding of your aptitude, which is derived from thoughtful introspection. We were chosen as finalists for the competition, receiving a modest capital infusion for our business. However, the prize money wasn't the principal benefit from the experience. What initially began as a résumé writing exercise blossomed into a lasting lesson on developing skills through our work.

Skill is the ability to do something well. It is a prowess or mastery birthed out of the intersection of desire and discipline. While vocational skills are of innumerable variety, I have discovered that four foundational skills are common to nearly all professions. These are *listening, visualizing, collaborating,* and *leading.* Each skill is unique and requires a distinct way of thinking. Your willingness to develop these skills determines your work productivity. I've learned over time that small changes in style and approach can lead to significant improvements in the level of effectiveness. You must continuously improve your skills to achieve professional success. It is equally important to know when to listen, visualize, collaborate, or lead. While these four foundational skills are not intended to be all-encompassing, they offer a sound framework to evaluate your occupational proficiency. We will explore each skill to identify distinct attributes and potential refinements that can enhance our work experience.

LISTENING

Listening is the first skill. All forms of work require the attainment, development, and application of specific competencies. Listening is consequently the most fundamental skill required for success. The key to being a good learner is being a good listener. Consequently, you must develop this vital skill to flourish in the workplace. You must be adept at listening to the needs of customers or clients. You must be attuned to listening to the feedback and critiques of coworkers and managers. More than simply hearing the words, effective listening requires a willingness to receive and a teachable demeanor. Early into my professional experience, I recognized I needed to significantly improve my listening skills if I hoped to maximize my professional opportunities. During difficult periods at work and in life, I focus more intently on this basic competency. How do you rate your listening skills? We are not formally taught the skill of listening. Therefore, most of us aren't inherently good listeners. With practice, we can significantly improve our listening skills, increasing our effectiveness in the process. Becoming a better listener makes us more effective workers and makes our work more enjoyable.

The first key for developing listening skills is preparing to listen. I am an extrovert and am inclined to process thoughts through verbal discourse. No one can, however, talk and listen at the same time. Moreover, it is easy to default to a mindset of simply waiting to speak. Silence does not necessarily equate to listening. Telling myself upfront that my primary focus is listening allows me to learn without the most likely interruptions, which are my own. That brings me to the next key. To listen effectively, you must remove distractions. This includes your favorite electronic devices. It also includes mental distractions like the recent disagreement with a coworker. Distractions rob us of listening opportunities and impede our development. The third key is offering others your undivided attention. My mother's teaching that to be attentive is a form of respect rings true. The final key is to remain curious. My father taught me that everyone has something to teach you if you are willing to listen. These simple keys will serve you well in the workplace if you apply them. Listening is a skill that only gets better with patience and practice.

VISUALIZING

The second skill is visualizing. During my career, I have been afforded a wide range of opportunities to conceptualize the future state of products, functions, and business lines. My responsibilities have included developing and executing operating plans. My responsibilities have also involved setting performance goals and objectives for others and myself. These experiences involve tapping into the human capacity to develop a vision for and path toward the future. I have not borne these responsibilities alone. I continue to have the good fortune of working alongside highly talented and motivated individuals who are committed to a shared mission. In ways big and small, all of us have the opportunity and even formal responsibility for contributing to the vision of an enterprise. Thus the act or process of visualizing is an important aspect of our work. Specifically, we must develop a mental picture of what we want our work product and our workplace to look like in the future. What ideas do you have for new products or services that can be provided to customers? What suggestions do you have about how your work can be performed more efficiently? What are your professional goals for the new year? What collective goals do you want to achieve with collaboration from coworkers? In order to realize tangible outcomes, you must first visualize them. To have a fulfilling work experience, you must first picture it in your mind. Visualization alone does not lead to tangible outcomes. It must be accompanied by planning and hands-on application. Visualization is, however, a valuable skill that allows us to connect our head and our hands, turning our ideas into action. With focus and practice, we can all become better at visualization.

The first key to developing visualizing skills is clearing the calendar. To be effective in this area, you need quiet time. These days we are inundated with electronic media and other stimuli that can create a false sense of urgency. Visualization sometimes requires us to unplug. Our never-ending to-do lists also crowd out visualizing. I've instituted the practice of regularly blocking out time on my schedule for visualization. I am most effective visualizing at the beginning and end of the workday. As such, I preserve those times whenever possible. The second key for visualization is to regularly feed your mind with information and perspectives that expand your knowledge and stretch your imagination. I am a voracious reader. I utilize various forms of electronic media and leverage the power of the internet. I also feed my mind through valuable conversations with subject matter experts and strategic thinkers. The final key is to organize your ideas and thoughts. I keep notebooks to capture my thoughts and review my ideas during my quiet times. I group my observations into important findings, new theorems, and open questions. Taken together, these keys will help you develop the skill of visualization.

COLLABORATING

Collaborating is the third skill. Collaboration involves working with others to achieve a common purpose. My work involves envisioning business strategies, developing innovative products, and devising distribution plans. This type of work requires creativity, and it nearly always involves partnering with others. Collaboration is a particular form of partnering and a vital skill in the modern workplace. Workers who hone the skill of collaborating are highly valuable because they facilitate the exchange of ideas and resources within organizations. The transfer of knowledge and the inclusion of diverse perspectives achieved through collaboration produce better outcomes. An equally important benefit of collaboration is that it strengthens relationships between coworkers. Individuals who are skilled at collaboration don't just produce better work. They have a more enjoyable experience.

The key to developing the skill of collaboration involves social maturity and the capacity to relate to others. A diverse group of collaborators produces better ideas and a richer experience. I advocate for this whenever I take on an assignment that involves collaborative work. My preparation also involves advance engagement with the working group members.

Positive connections with team members prior to active engagement helps you work collaboratively. The next key involves filling your emotional tank. It may be something as simple as taking a quick walk to get some fresh air or reflecting on prior team successes. Collaboration requires positive emotional energy, so it helps to begin with a full tank.

The final step involves the environment and timing. The choice of time and place can have a material impact on the quality of collaboration. I'm naturally a morning person and do my best collaborative work in the first half of the day. I have also found shifting the location to a less formal communal space creates an environment conducive to partnering.

Collaboration in its highest form involves the capacity to recognize the different personalities and talents among individuals and how the group can work together to achieve the best outcome. Not every individual excels in this area, and some people have a distinctive ability to foster great teamwork. Allowing these individuals to use their gift is another way of developing your own capacity for collaboration. Cultivating the skill of collaboration materially improves your work experience.

LEADING

Leading is the fourth and final skill. If you work as part of a team, the individual contributions must be coordinated. Whether positional leadership or informal leadership, opportunities arise to serve the mission by organizing, conducting, or directing the efforts of others. In most cases, our leadership responsibilities are not formal. In fact, we seamlessly flow from leadership roles to support roles as situations require. There is an age-old debate as to whether leaders are born or made. I believe each of us has the capacity to lead. This potential is something we all are born with. The skill of leading, however, requires the right attitude and aptitude and therefore is mostly made. This is an encouraging observation because it affirms we all can develop the skill of leading whatever our mix of innate abilities. Leading is principally about positive influence. Positional authority is not a requirement for leading. We can lead from whatever position we are in. An important aspect of developing the skill of leadership is recognizing the situations that call for our special brand of leadership. Equally important is recognizing the situations that call for us to be effective followers.

The first key to developing the skill of leading is to affirm the objective or mission. Coworkers are motivated and united by a shared mission. You must have a clear understanding of the mission to be an effective leader. The next step is to give yourself a prep talk. This differs from a pep talk. You cannot effectively lead with an inflated or sensitive ego. Being secure with yourself is key to adopting the proper attitude to lead others. The next key is to identify specific ways to ensure the success of your team members. It is one thing to claim to be a servant leader. It is far better to let your actions speak for you. The final key is to seek feedback. I've often heard it said that leadership is lonely. This is particularly the case if we approach leadership opportunities as a lone wolf. The skill of leading is valuable to any effort, and your coworkers are invested in your success. An effective leader has both the wisdom and humility to seek perspective and counsel from their coworkers. These simple actions can help you develop as a leader. You have the capacity to lead. Work provides countless opportunities for you to show it.

DO YOU HAVE SKILLS?

In the first section of the book I provided a construct for aptitude that apportioned talent into two buckets: natural abilities and acquired competencies. My natural abilities include adeptness in creative thinking, problem solving, and both written and oral communication. My acquired skills include proficiency in financial analysis, business development, and team leadership. I process information by strategizing options and manage uncertainty by innovating. My work has given me the opportunity to develop these abilities and competencies to increasing levels of expertise. These are a subset of the skills that enable my vocational pursuits. As noted earlier, we tend to give a great percentage of our waking hours to work or vocation-related pursuits. And since time is our most valuable resource, we owe it to ourselves to make our investment of time and talent count. Innate talent alone is not sufficient to maximize our potential. Our talent must be developed to the point of great prowess and proficiency.

Work increases and develops your skills. Professional development is one of the most valuable aspects of your vocational experience. Your skills reflect not only what you can produce through your work but also what your work has perfected in you. Thomas Davidson, a nineteenth-century philosopher, stated, "What you are will show in what you do."[1] Who you are, with respect to your values, and what you are, with respect to your virtues, is ultimately revealed by what you do in life. Your life's work testifies your skills have been put to good use. To do work that matters and to produce work products of value, you must develop skills. Becoming highly skilled is one of the surest proofs you have a genuine work ethic. Your skillset is also evidence of both the kind of person you are and the quality of work you do. Building your skills will ensure your work contributions are valued and you find joy in the work you do.

CHAPTER 11 REFLECTIONS

Work Develops Skill

———

KEY INSIGHTS

- Skill is prowess or mastery that is birthed out of the intersection of desire and discipline.

- Four key skills—listening, visualizing, collaborating, and leading—are fundamental to success.

- Listening entails removing distractions, being attentive, and remaining engaged.

- Visualizing requires clearing your calendar; feeding your mind with fresh information and diverse perspectives; and organizing your ideas and thoughts.

- Collaborating involves honing your relationship skills, which allows you to facilitate the exchange of ideas and resources with others.

- Leading is principally about positive influence. You must articulate a shared mission, prepare mentally, ensure the success of others, and constantly seek feedback.

- Positional authority is not a requirement for leadership; lead from any position.

WORK FOSTERS RELATIONSHIPS

*Unity is strength. When there is teamwork and
collaboration, wonderful things can be achieved.*

MATTIE J.T. STEPANEK

I read an article in the Harvard Business Review written
by Paul Zak that provided an insightful perspective on workplace relationships.[1] While a variety of factors lead to disengagement by workers, the article identifies the lack of trust as a
root cause. Trust is defined as the confidence we place in the
ability, character, and intent of another person. Trust is the basis
of every healthy relationship. People perform better and are
happier when they do meaningful work with people they trust.
There is a body of emerging research that empirically measures
return on trust. Similar to evaluating operating or financial metrics,
researchers use employee surveys to measure the impact of specific
behaviors on corporate culture. This type of research not only
sheds light on the quality of employee engagement but also identifies action steps that will increase trust among coworkers. The
article highlights a survey of approximately 1,100 US workers. A
composite score was computed to measure the level of trust at
the subject companies. The companies were then grouped into

quartiles with the lowest quartile compared to the highest quartile to draw inferences. Responses of workers from top quartile companies were demonstrably different from bottom quartile companies. Top-quartile company workers reported being 50 percent more productive, 76 percent more engaged, and twice as energetic. The research suggests employers can dramatically increase productivity by cultivating a culture of trust, and workers can significantly improve their work experience by building trusting relationships. The clear implication of the findings is that workers from "high trust" companies find greater joy in their work.

How do leaders of the most trusted companies achieve greater trust? An overarching theme is that their approach is varied and intentional. While the article enumerated a number of leadership actions, I will highlight three in particular. The first behavior is encouraging workers to intentionally build relationships with their colleagues. People trust people they know. Trusted leaders model this behavior by being personally accessible and creating opportunities for coworkers to get to know one another. The second behavior is ensuring information is shared broadly among workers. Transparency encourages and improves communication throughout the organization. Workers armed with complete and accurate information are more apt to act in the best interest of the collective, which increases the level of trust within the culture. The third behavior is showing vulnerability. Sharing concerns, admitting mistakes, and asking for help demonstrate vulnerability. This behavior helps remove barriers to trust, increasing empathy among coworkers. Each of the highlighted behaviors contributes to improving the depth and quality of interactions. This leads to a more essential revelation: work, done well, fosters genuine relationships.

THE THREEFOLD CORD

Whoever coined the phrase "variety is the spice of life" must have had human relationships in mind. New and exciting experiences with diverse people make our lives more interesting. Each of our lives is fuller and richer because of the people we've come to know. Living in community and forming close relationships with others epitomizes what it means to be human. The people we form connections with influence our character and behavior. Our work is integral to our lives and plays a big role in our socialization. We dedicate many of our waking hours to our vocation, exerting significant emotional energy in the process. An underappreciated aspect of our vocational pursuits is the impact it has on our human relationships. Our work not only affects existing relationships but prompts new relationships. Work fosters relationships in three primary ways. First, work compels us to *commit* to a shared mission, aligning our interests with others. Next, work allows us to *connect* with people we don't know and may have never met. Finally, work encourages us to *communicate* with others to share knowledge and exchange ideas.

Several years ago, I became aware of the personal narrative of an exceptional individual who truly added spice to life. Matthew Stepanek was born with dysautonomic mitochondrial myopathy, a rare neuromuscular disorder.[2] This genetic condition causes damage to mitochondria, which are the energy producing parts of the cells that make up our bodies. Symptoms of the disorder include poor growth, muscle weakness, learning disabilities, and a number of other diseases and physical ailments. Treatment is limited, and the disorder often results in premature death. Mattie, as he was commonly known, faced another significant challenge when his parents separated during his early childhood. Mattie's disease did not define his destiny nor did his circumstances hinder the indelible mark he made on the world. From a very young age, Mattie was acquainted with great work. He demonstrated an uncommon level of maturity and wisdom for someone so young. You might say he was an old soul. Mattie became a philosopher, speaker, and poet, publishing seven bestselling books of poetry. Oprah

Winfrey described him as a messenger for our times. His personal hero, Jimmy Carter, described him simply as the most extraordinary person he has ever known. Mattie accomplished all of this prior to his early death at the age of thirteen.

As a philosopher, Mattie offered thoughtful perspectives on a great many topics, including work. In particular, he espoused the vital importance of collaborative relationships. Mattie believed that unity and teamwork enabled people to accomplish incredible feats. Unity involves joining together to achieve a purpose. This oneness or strength is the result of harmonious relationships. We may independently accomplish significant feats. However, as Mattie perceptively observed, we can achieve extraordinary things when we team up with others. Consider the wisdom of King Solomon.

> Two are better than one,
>   because they have a good return for their labor:
> If either of them falls down,
>   one can help the other up. . . .
> Though one may be overpowered,
>   two can defend themselves.
> A cord of three strands is not quickly broken. (Eccles 4:9-12)

It seems both Solomon and Mattie agree on two important principles. In unity, there is strength. Additionally, great things are accomplished through collaborative working relationships. The achievements or rewards generally come in the form of greater productivity and deeper fellowship. The relationships we foster are arguably the most enduring reward. Let's delve further into how the threefold cord of commitment, connection, and collaboration fosters relationships.

BEING COMMITTED

The very nature of work encourages people to join together in pursuit of a common mission. A distinguishing characteristic of engaged employees is their commitment to the organizational mission. Commitment occurs when common interests supersede individual preferences. What goes around relationally does indeed come around. When we commit to the success of our coworkers, they respond in kind. What does commitment to coworkers look like in practice? True commitment requires us to cultivate harmonious relationships with coworkers. In order to achieve this, we must treat our coworkers respectfully. Commitment requires us to trust our coworkers' abilities and intentions. We must seek to help our coworkers as opposed to change them. Commitment also involves taking accountability for shared responsibilities as well as any issues that arise. When we are committed to the success of our coworkers, we make every effort to constructively resolve conflicts. Our commitment to our colleagues is what makes work, well, *work*.

During my career, I have worked alongside dedicated professionals forging relationships through commitments to one another. One of the experiences that had a significant impact on me involved launching a new business segment for the company. I have spent a good portion of my career working in asset management, providing investment solutions to institutions and individuals. A growth segment of the industry involves the development and distribution of investment products known as exchange-traded funds. I was charged with assembling a team to devise a strategy— and ultimately design and distribute—a family of fund products. This involved a wide-ranging set of milestones, including getting approval from regulatory agencies, attracting capital, and developing marketing and sales plans. After receiving my mandate, I set about the task of a de novo build. I was initially assigned two senior professionals within the company to work on the new initiative. Next, I recruited and hired additional senior managers responsible for key functional areas of the business. Our senior team did not have any preexisting association, so we had to learn to work as a team. I initially focused on leading the development of the vision and strategy. From there, we articulated and executed against measurable objectives. I would love to tell you it was easy, but that is far from the truth. Pursuing a compelling vision never is. The storms were recurrent events during our forming, storming, norming, and performing stages of team formation.[3] There were not only pressures within our group, but we faced the challenges of integrating new partners into broader corporate culture. Not the least of our worries was the growing competition in our highly competitive market segment. In the midst of these dynamic forces, our group persevered.

Two things were evident with our group from the very start. First, our team worked tirelessly. We were passionate and persistent in our approach. Second, we were very adept at problem solving. Whether by creative thinking or steadfast perseverance, the team continually overcame challenges. Our diligent efforts were accompanied by a bit of grace and good timing, which led to commercial success. The success was increasingly recognized inside and outside of the company. My privilege as the founding member of the group provided me with a unique perspective. From this perch, I observed something truly special. Our diverse group had become a high performing team. Were we perfect? Hardly. Were we effective? Definitely! We were effective primarily due to our commitment to a shared vision and ultimately because of our commitments to one another. Our relationships grew professionally and personally as a result of our mutual commitments.

GETTING CONNECTED

Our natural human instinct is to connect with other people. Neuroscience reveals that humans are not only uniquely relational, but our social environment profoundly shapes us. Research has also shown that our social connections affect our physical and emotional health. Positive social connections strengthen the immune system, improve self-esteem, and lead to longer lives. Conversely, a lack of social connectedness leads to a decline in physical and psychological health and a high propensity for antisocial behavior. Our bodies and our minds consciously and unconsciously affirm, *Relationships matter*. When we initiate and maintain positive relationships with others, we are more productive and more fulfilled. This reality is abundantly clear as it pertains to work. I've often observed that my most enjoyable and productive experiences involved working on highly functional teams. In fact, I have maintained close connections with those team members long after the completion of our work. I am blessed to have a breadth of personal relationships forged in the crucible of work.

I began my career as an analyst working for a Wall Street firm. I was literally and figuratively a far cry from my Southside Chicago home. I quickly learned to appreciate how work connects us with new and interesting people. I had the good fortune of joining alongside a small cohort of fellow analysts who hailed from very diverse backgrounds. Niko was my first acquaintance and became a very dear friend. He had emigrated to the United States from an Eastern European country during high school. Although we grew up worlds apart, we shared commonalities in our upbringing that shaped our life experiences. Manabu was an expatriate from Japan living in the United States for the first time. I served as cultural coach, helping him understand aspects of the language and culture. He in turn taught me a great deal about Eastern culture. Andy hailed from an affluent family in the Northeast. Several of his close relatives worked on Wall Street. He shared helpful insights on the Wall Street subculture. I returned the favor by sharing my knowledge of financial analysis and modeling, as I was the resident accounting-degree holder among our cohort.

The first year on the job was a crash course as we learned functional responsibilities and navigated a new culture. We typically worked thirteen-hour days and spent most of our waking hours with one another. We grew close as a cohort, including socializing outside of work. We not only grew together professionally, we learned a great deal from our respective personal experiences. The opportunity to become connected to these individuals through my work was a valuable life experience. Meaningful professional growth resulted from the relationships formed. Work was the conduit for establishing these connections, which otherwise were unlikely to occur. The capacity for our work to create new connections that foster valued relationships is a benefit we should not take for granted. One of the ways to measure meaningfulness in our work is to assess the connections we have made along the way. When this occurs, we have doubly won because both our work and our relationships bring us joy.

COMMUNICATING EFFECTIVELY

Brian Tracy, an authority on the development of human potential, says positive emotional energy is the key to happiness in life.[4] While my faith is the ultimate source of my joy, my emotional state indeed impacts how I experience all aspects of life—including work. Work requires us to act in concert with others to be productive. Therefore, effective communication is an essential ingredient for success in most vocations. The benefit of communicating effectively goes beyond simply producing great work. The most enduring result of good communication is the cultivation of professional and personal relationships. Good communicators make work more enjoyable by fostering healthy relationships. The ability to communicate effectively generates positive emotional energy in your work life. Communicating effectively doesn't always come easily. Conflicts inevitably arise. Good communicators become skilled at conflict resolution. You must compromise and even concede certain positions to maintain open lines of communication. Above all else, effective communication requires a listening ear. Showing empathy is essential for sustaining healthy working relationships, which leads to discovering joy in work.

One of my more meaningful work efforts was spurred by a personal passion. About sixteen years ago, I volunteered with a friend to provide basic education in the area of personal finance. We partnered with a community bank as well as other non-profit organizations to provide free seminars. We relished the opportunity to share our acquired expertise with underserved communities. Another of my passions from my youth is writing. Inspired by the nature of our volunteer work, I decided to write a book on personal finance. My first step involved drafting a detailed outline and project summary. I determined I had outlined not one but two books. An unconventional idea came to mind. I pitched my friend on coauthoring a two-part series where he would author one of the two books. Specifically, we set out to concurrently write books that would form a cohesive series. This was an ambitious undertaking for two first-time authors, but we frankly didn't know any better.

You may know the quip that we can sing at the same time, but we can't talk at the same time. We learned from our experience we could write at the same time, but it took quite a bit of communication. The first and most relevant thing we learned was we have opposite temperament types and communication styles. I am an abstract communicator and he is a concrete communicator. We grew to appreciate our differences and eventually benefitted from the habits and perspectives we shared with one another. Effective communication requires the appreciation and assimilation of differences. The second lesson involved synchronization. The desired end product required continuity between the two works. Even our commonly held views had to be harmonized. Finally, communication is iterative. We had to constantly and painstakingly compare notes to ensure we were intellectually consistent and avoided redundancy. We quickly understood why some artists bolt from the group and go solo. Inasmuch as it was our maiden voyage as writers, we had much to learn and perfect. I still do.

However, there were two certain outcomes that resulted from the level of communication required. The work product was better, and our relationship grew stronger.

COMIC RELIEF

Dilbert is an American comic strip known for its satirical office humor featuring an engineer at a technology company as the title character.[5] The strip portrays corporate culture as an environment where bureaucracy and office politics get in the way of productivity and genuine relationships. The comic strip, which is written and illustrated by Scott Adams, has persisted for nearly three decades, drawing an unusually large following in business and popular culture. Dilbert appears in two thousand newspapers worldwide in sixty-five countries and twenty-five languages. The popular success is undoubtedly attributable to its workplace themes, which often highlight common relational issues. The comic strip features several recurring characters including Dilbert's cunning pet dog, his overbearing boss, an assertive coworker, and Catbert, a fictional cat who serves as the dubious director of human resources. A familiar idiom says that many a true word is spoken in jest. Adams regularly strikes this chord with readers through his satirical comic strip. In particular, his cynical truth sheds light on relationships among coworkers.

I was recently thumbing through the newspaper when I came across a timely Dilbert comic strip.[6] This submission featured his straitlaced manager and Catbert, the human resources director. The manager remarks he has been telling fellow employees their culture was their best asset. Catbert cynically asks, "Do they pretend that makes sense?" The manager replies the employees go along with his claim because in their culture, employees lie to avoid conflict. This type of duplicity is observed in corporate cultures far more frequently than people admit. This behavior is also in stark contrast to the "high trust" cultures highlighted at the beginning of the chapter. In a culture founded upon trusting relationships, employees do not feel compelled to lie to avoid conflict. Employees who trust one another are transparent and constructively address conflicts. Great work relationships are often formed or solidified in the midst of conflict. The result is, however, well worth the effort. When our work—and, moreover, our working relationships—truly matter, culture indeed becomes a prized asset.

We've cited research from the Gallup Organization and on several occasions given their insights on the attitudes and behaviors of workers globally. A simple yet telling research finding ties directly to our exploration of work relationships. People who work with someone they consider a good friend are more fulfilled in their work. Moreover, just one good friendship increases employees' level of creativity, productivity, and accountability at work. This finding should not come as a surprise. We instinctively seek positive interactions and social connections in every facet of our lives. Work provides you with ample opportunities to establish meaningful relationships with coworkers, customers, suppliers, and other stakeholders. The better your relationships are, the happier you're going to be. You get a special feeling when you foster relationships through commitment, connection, and communication. That feeling is the satisfaction of discovering joy in your work.

CHAPTER 12 REFLECTIONS

Work Fosters Relationships

———

KEY INSIGHTS

- Improve your work experience by building trusting relationships. Trust is built by committing to a shared mission, communicating regularly, and connecting personally with coworkers.

- Transparency encourages and improves communication within groups. Sharing complete information and candid perspectives increases the level of trust among coworkers.

- Sharing your concerns, admitting your mistakes, and asking others for help shows vulnerability and removes barriers to trust.

- Commitment requires trust in your coworkers' abilities and intentions. Seek to help your coworkers as opposed to trying to change them.

- One of the ways to measure the meaningfulness of work is to assess your personal connections. Work allows you to cultivate meaningful professional and personal relationships.

- Communicating effectively doesn't always come easily as conflicts inevitably arise. Compromise, and even concede certain positions, to maintain open lines of communication.

- Your vocation provides opportunities to develop relationships that transcend the workplace. The better your relationships, the happier you will be.

13

WORK PRODUCES VALUE

Far and away the best prize life has to offer is the
chance to work hard at work worth doing.

THEODORE ROOSEVELT

In physics, work is the result of a force acting on an object and moving it by a quantifiable distance. The work performed is measured by the degree of movement. We learn several truths from this simple equation. First, we observe work is the result of effort. Work occurs only when force is applied. Second, there must be an object or objective to which our effort is applied. Whether capitalizing on an opportunity or solving a problem, work demands a focused effort. Third, there is tangible evidence when real work is performed. Work is not identified with activity but rather with progress or results. The surest evidence of work done well is the achievement of the desired outcome. Real work results in value in the form of desired benefits, useful products, needed services, increased utility, or greater worth. Like the distance in our physics equation, the value is measurable. This truth directly relates to the fundamental principle of this chapter. Work produces value.

During the early part of my career, I worked in the capital markets divisions of two prominent investment banking firms. I enjoyed my work and the people I worked with. The company described our work environment as "entrepreneurial" and employees were encouraged to "act like owners." This refrain took on a whole new meaning when I ventured out from the corporate umbrella to start a small business with a dear friend. Our principal business was a specialty retailer that sold books, curriculum, supplies, and music. We had a physical location and an online presence. We also had related business activities including an independent publishing imprint. Contrary to popular opinion, business ownership is not so much about being the boss. It does, however, involve personal sacrifice and accountability. My business partner and I served as the founders, financiers, managers, and initial employees of our company. The only way work got done was if we did it. There was little talk of sick days or benefits. Our conversations and efforts focused squarely on creating value for our stakeholders. This mindset informed our managerial, operational, and developmental practices.

In the early days of our fledgling business, we realized the vital need to create value. Our employees took greater accountability for the business results and their vocational development when their efforts were linked to value creation. A quote Theodore Roosevelt Jr. passed along from an acquaintance invoked the spirit of accountability we sought to embody. "Do what you can, with what you have, where you are."[1] I posted it on the door of our shared space that served as the office and break room. The quote was generally the first and last thing we saw each business day. As novice operators, we didn't have deep experience to draw from. We did, however, take three important steps vital in our pursuit of value. First, we set clear goals tied to value creation for our stakeholders. Second, we disaggregated the goals into specific objectives that reflected the financial and nonfinancial results we aimed to achieve. Third, we established key performance measures we routinely reviewed and published. These performance measures were linked to the value drivers of the business and reflected the health of the business and level of value creation. Taken together, these steps focused our efforts on value creation.

MEASURING UP

As an entrepreneur, you receive constant feedback from employees, customers, and other stakeholders as to whether and how you create value (not to mention the bottom line results reflected in the profit and loss statement). Activity and value creation are not the same. Likewise, not everything we can readily count reflects long-term value. Entrepreneurs quickly learn their paychecks are not a useful measure for value creation. Compensation often provides a diminished or exaggerated view of work contribution. Successful entrepreneurs routinely delay consumption and gratification in pursuit of their vision. Real value is measured by factors such as employee engagement, customer loyalty, vendor relationships, community development, and profitability. These value measurements exist for businesses of virtually all sizes and scales. And while the economic contribution of a business may be relatively small, the value delivered to stakeholders can be quite large with the proper focus.

If you talk to entrepreneurs long enough, they are bound to tell you about their troubled ventures. The quip "nothing ventured, nothing gained" was likely coined by an entrepreneur. Running a small business was one of my most challenging professional experiences. I would love to report that our entrepreneurial endeavors yielded great commercial success. That was not, however, our plight. After five years we closed our retail business. When a business closes, the common refrain is that it was a failure. This is, however, the view of those detached from the actual experience. My experience was by no means a failure. My years as a retail business owner—and moreover as a founder and owner of several small businesses—afforded me invaluable lessons. Chief among these is the fundamental understanding that real work produces value. These experiences complemented my other vocational experiences. Through entrepreneurship I discovered a renewed joy in work, a joy that comes from inwardly knowing one's work is valued and is valuable.

VALUE MATTERS

In our modern economy, elements of work are increasingly distributed and specialized. This creates great efficiencies and economies of scale for manufacturing and service industries alike. Individual contributions are broken down into parts, and work is generally associated with an activity or job. Their contribution also is often measured and remunerated based on their level of activity. For example, I was once employed as a medical records clerk during my summer break from college. I spent the entire summer updating and filing medical records. I never had any perspective of how my efforts contributed to the greater objectives of the hospital or how I helped to serve patients. My efforts were measured and rewarded by the number of files I processed. This parsing of work produces economic benefit, allowing successive generations to consume more per capita in the form of goods and services. There is, however, a trade-off. The nature of modern work often dissociates workers from the final work product and beneficiary of their effort. Value creation also comes in the form of incremental improvements workers make in performing their assigned tasks. Workers often are unable to see the value of their particular contribution to the overall process. Workers are therefore less aware, and in many instances, less concerned about real value creation.

As it pertains to work, value matters. Our physics equation taught us that work is evidenced by distance traveled. Distance in this equation is synonymous with value. It is difficult to discover joy in one's work without a sense of accomplishment. Effort is essential. However, effort alone does not give us joy. In fact, we observe quite the opposite. Continuous effort without achievement is discouraging. We have an inherent need to understand the value created by our work. The value we create gives our work meaning and makes us feel valued for our contributions. The value we create is shared by others generating tangible and intangible benefits. Earlier, I referenced three tactics employed during my first entrepreneurial experience. We will explore each of these more expressly as they reveal invaluable lessons pertaining to value creation.

CLEAR GOALS

For work to take place, an object has to move some distance. The object in our equation is synonymous with a goal. Goals are what we might refer to as the big rocks that must be moved, an intended outcome that is clearly identified. Clarity by itself does not lead to value creation. Goals must be set in the context of shared mission and values. There is always a risk that goals may be unwise or unreasonable. Continually aligning goals with a common mission and shared values helps discern whether they are admirable and worth pursuing. Goal setting is practically addressed by answering three simple questions: Which opportunities will you pursue? What problems will you solve? How will you serve others? You have a unique perspective that allows you to see opportunities others may not see. You can solve problems proximate to you by applying your distinctive insights. You can help others to flourish through serving and leading in specific ways. When you set clear goals in these areas, you are able to create value through your work. In my example, we acquired an existing retail business. The financial position was deteriorating quickly, and we needed to make changes. The establishment of clear goals helped us turn our financial situation around and set us on a course to maximizing value.

After surveying our stakeholders, three goals came into view. The first goal related to our employees. Our employees had received little

in the way of training and had very little autonomy to make basic
decisions. They were in the best position to improve the customer
experience and tackle daily problems but lacked the skills and encouragement to do so. Our first goal was to empower our employees.
The second goal related to our customers. We needed more loyal
customers. Loyal customers are repeat buyers and refer other customers. We had the technology and means to capture and analyze
customer behavior, but it was underutilized. We set out to profile
our customers and ultimately tailor our offering and services. This
would enable us to achieve our goal of cultivating more loyal customers. The third goal related to vendor management. We simply
had too many vendors given the scale of the business. As a result,
we were not proactively engaging vendors. This resulted in missed
opportunities for discounts and promotions as well as inventory
shortages. Our third goal was to excel at vendor management.

SPECIFIC OBJECTIVES

A goal may be disaggregated into multiple objectives. An objective is a specific result we seek to achieve. The pursuit of objectives guides our efforts and enables us to achieve our overarching
goals. Objectives are determined relative to time and resource
constraints. As such, they are more readily measured and serve as
the basis for evaluating performance. Examples of work objectives
include improving service quality, acquiring new customers, and
reducing expenditures. Defining specific objectives creates the
conditions for productive work to take place because intent must
be translated into action. Achieving specific objectives allows us
to see our progress on the way toward our greater goals, giving us
a sense of accomplishment in our work. This pride in work well
done reinforces our efforts because our achievements are visible.
Achieving specific objectives also leads to value creation.

With clear goals in hand, we turned our attention to determining specific objectives. We set goals related to employee

empowerment, customer engagement, and vendor management. With respect to employee empowerment, we focused on training and development. The objectives were based on the hours dedicated to training as well as effectiveness on specific competencies. We found increased skills led to improved aptitude and attitude. With respect to customer engagement, we instituted a loyalty programs for retail customers and institutional buyers, offering preferred terms and special services. We set objectives related to number of store visits, purchases per month, average ticket size, and satisfaction ratings. Customers responded positively to our focus on engagement. With respect to vendor management, we set objectives for inventory turns, average purchase discounts, and inventory days payable. Setting specific objectives allowed us to shift from a reactive to a proactive approach to vendor engagement. Vendors appreciated the transparent approach, and we were better able to manage inevitable discrepancies and conflicts.

PERFORMANCE MEASURES

A performance measure is a standard of measurement by which efficiency, progress, or quality can be assessed. In the context of business or work, it is a quantifiable indicator used to assess how well an organization or business is achieving its objectives. In order to achieve business goals, we must determine and complete specific objectives. Value creation is measurable. Defining and reviewing performance measures is a way of keeping score. Performance measures provide an objective assessment of the health of the business and indicate whether improvement is needed. The measures reveal whether we are creating value. To win a game you have to keep score. This is also true as it pertains to work. Measuring performance is the means by which we keep score. Keeping score involves not only measuring results but also critically assessing performance in light of the results. It is also important that everyone on the team is involved in keeping score and not just management. To make sure goals are clear and attainable, businesses often employ goal-setting frameworks. SMART is a useful acronym that guides goal setting. The criteria prescribes that goals need to be *specific, measurable, achievable, relevant*, and *time-based*.[2] With clear goals and specific objectives established, we turned our attention to performance measures. My partner was particularly adept at measurement and reporting. He created a simple scorecard that enumerated and tracked key performance measures. During our monthly meetings with employees, we regularly reviewed performance through the lens of the scorecard. We took care to relate the measures to daily activities and employee actions. For example, we articulated how an additional small purchase by a loyal customer during a regular visit impacted the profitability of the store. This was associated with specific skills developed in sales training. An example was using the customer data in our point-of-sale system to ensure desired items were in stock. The same data was also used to recommend items that fit customer preferences. Many individuals incorrectly view keeping score as mundane. In practice, we found our employees looked forward to gaining insights about the business. This also enabled them to provide valuable insights into what should be measured and how we could better drive performance. Finally, we created a basic profit-sharing program linked to the performance measures. All employees participated in the value creation of the business due to the establishment of performance measures.

THE VALUE OF HARD WORK

Theodore Roosevelt Jr. is considered one of the most influential political leaders in the history of the United States of America. This is why his likeness is preserved on Mount Rushmore alongside George Washington, Thomas Jefferson, and Abraham Lincoln. One of the things that distinguished Roosevelt was his attitude and approach to work.[3] Roosevelt was born a sickly child with a debilitating case of asthma. He did not, however, succumb to his illness but instead worked himself into strong physical condition. He was a man of many interests and pursued varied vocations before diving headlong into a political career. Roosevelt was a writer, historian, naval administrator, deputy sheriff, hunter, and rancher. His experiences ranged from writing a history book to leading the Rough Riders during the Spanish-American war. We can safely say he knew a thing or two about varied forms of work. By virtue of his experiences, Roosevelt practically understood that real work produces value.

I have worked as a volunteer, laborer, specialist, executive, and entrepreneur. Each experience has provided unique lessons concerning work and life. My work as an entrepreneur revealed three fundamental steps for producing value through work. The first step is to establish clear goals. Work is not intended to be an aimless endeavor. Your work will prove most rewarding if you achieve clearly defined goals. And while you may contribute to shared goals, it is equally important you set personal goals for producing value. The second step involves pursuing specific objectives. If you want to launch a new initiative or start your own business, begin with a specific objective such as researching your target market. Objectives direct your plans and focus your efforts. Your third and final step is to measure your performance. Many individuals become preoccupied with the busyness of the workplace. But real work produces valuable outcomes. Value is quantifiable in most instances; therefore, it is important to keep score. Creating value through work is one of the greatest joys life offers.

Like Roosevelt, I have experienced the joy of working hard at work worth doing. This value has been actualized in clients served, employees developed, communities impacted, and profits generated. The vocational and life skills I have acquired are immensely valuable. The distance traveled is reflected in my own personal and professional development. The distance traveled is reflected in the relationships forged with others, which continue to result in collaboration and value creation. The distance traveled is reflected in the expansion and evolution of business enterprises that exist solely because of the commitment of coworkers to a shared mission. Taken together, all these distances traveled reflect the unique value I have contributed through my work. Similarly, you have a lifelong track record of distances traveled. This distance or value is your lasting gift to those served through your work. You know value when you see it. As Roosevelt wisely asserted, meaningful work is worthwhile. It offers the kind of joy each of us must endeavor to discover in our life's journey.

Work Produces Value

KEY INSIGHTS

- Work translates your physical, mental, and emotional effort into tangible value.

- Real work produces value in the form of desired benefits, useful products, needed services, increased utility, or greater worth.

- Determine value by answering three simple questions: Which opportunities will you pursue? What problems will you solve? How will you serve others?

- Setting clear goals, disaggregating goals into specific objectives, and establishing performance measures translate effort into lasting value.

- Work proves most rewarding when you set and achieve clearly defined goals.

- Setting specific objectives guides your efforts and provides a basis for evaluating your performance.

- Measuring your performance provides you with means to understand the value of your work. Creating value through your work is one of the greatest joys in life.

14

WORK GLORIFIES GOD

There is always the danger that we may just do the work for the sake of the work. This is where the respect and the love and the devotion come in—that we do it to God, to Christ, and that's why we try to do it as beautifully as possible.

MOTHER TERESA

During my senior year of high school, I participated in a work-study program designed for students interested in careers in business. The prerequisites for the program included courses in accounting, economics, and typing. I began my school day early, which permitted a half-day work schedule with a major accounting firm. The program afforded three principal benefits. First, I received early career exposure and mentorship. The professionals I worked with taught me business concepts and professional etiquette. Second, I developed beneficial work habits and routines. I was required to develop personal discipline to balance a full course load and a 20-hour workweek. This experience proved invaluable during my transition to young adulthood. The third benefit was the income I earned. I made enough money to cover my discretionary expenses, which eased the financial load on my parents. I even saved up enough money to purchase a used car. The overall experience improved my financial acumen and boosted my self-esteem.

My work-study opportunity coincided with a fresh career start for my mother, whose faith and determination serve as a constant source of inspiration. Though a promising student, she dropped out of high school. She resumed her education later in life, receiving her bachelor and master's degrees. These stepping stones enabled her to pursue her lifelong calling to the field of social services. As fate would have it, both mother and son were embarking on new work experiences. She worked for a social services agency that focused on serving disadvantaged children. The children she served were often neglected. The physical and emotional abuse many endured was inconceivable. Her office was located in a crime-ridden neighborhood in the inner city. My father worked an evening shift, so it was my responsibility to pick my mother up from work. I looked forward to our one-on-one time following our respective workdays.

During our drive home one evening, I asked my mother about her career choice. Her clients were wards of the court. Their custody was entrusted to welfare agencies including the agency where she was employed. This resulted in transient living situations. Despite herculean efforts by agency staff, many clients failed to overcome their debilitating circumstances. Her agency was beset by resource constraints and funding shortfalls. This impacted the level and consistency of service clients received. The crime in the surrounding areas of her office was on the rise. Several staff members were, in fact, victims of offenses. From my perspective, this was a very difficult way to earn a living. "Son," she replied, "most of the young people I serve are abused or neglected. They often feel as if their lives don't matter and no one cares about them. Their lives do matter. They matter to God and they matter to me." Unsurprisingly, my mother's faith served as the basis of her commitment. She referenced a passage of Scripture that encourages people to give their whole heart to their work, serving others as if they are serving God. "The obstacles my clients face, and the job itself, can be overwhelming at times. Yet I know that my work is a blessing from the Lord." Her clarity of calling provided meaningfulness in her work. The alignment of her vocation and her life's purpose enabled her to find joy in the midst of difficult circumstances.

TO GOD BE THE GLORY

I pursued my career in finance with a tenacity and determination instilled by my parents. I naturally desired to excel in my vocation and purposefully went about mastering competencies related to my field. By common measures, I achieved early career success. This included frequent promotions, greater responsibility, and increased pay. I received favorable recognition from customers, colleagues, and supervisors. It was as if light was being shined on my abilities and accomplishments. While these accolades boosted my self-image, the puzzle remained incomplete. There was a light missing. This light is revealed when our work intersects with our purpose. I reflected on the lessons my mother taught in word and deed. Her sense of purpose and fulfillment was not gained through self-interest. We are taught that success and happiness come as a result of our individual accomplishments being recognized, but it turns out lasting joy comes by shining reflected light. She selflessly sought to glorify God in her work, finding success and joy in the process. The abiding sense of joy I sought required less of me. Likewise, the abiding sense of joy you seek requires less of you.

Something glorious and divine exists inside of each of us. Our work provides a means of letting our light shine in a way in which others can see it. God is glorified through our work when we demonstrate clarity of purpose, maturity of character, and excellence of achievement. Not only does our work speak, but our world is also made better. We instinctively know when God is glorified through our work because it coincides with achievements when we think of ourselves less. I recall volunteering at a Feed My Starving

Children packing event where our task was to assemble meal packages for distribution to disadvantaged people around the world.[1] The most memorable part of the day was when the organizers reported our results. The totals were reported in terms of the number of children that would be fed as a result of the day's work. When our totals were read, I sensed God was glorified. Similarly, I recall another work experience during my time as a proprietor of a small retail business. We were struggling financially and needed a major turnaround by year-end to stay in business. We executed a novel transaction that allowed us to remain in business. This preserved the jobs of those we employed as well as the services we provided to the community. I sensed God was glorified by our commitment to serve our employees and customers. This type of glory only comes when we focus on doing good as opposed to looking good.

You have heard the adage "actions speak louder than words." *Glorify* is a verb, or action word. We must put it into practice by means of a three-dimensional application. The first dimension is to honor God by demonstrating a high regard for every aspect of our work. What more appropriate way to honor God than by the nature and level of our commitment to work. The second dimension is to thank God for our opportunity to work. The ability to pursue meaningful work is a blessing. There is, in truth, a unique kind of joy we only find in our work. We tangibly show our appreciation by serving humanity through our work. Work provides the means to pay our gratitude forward. The third dimension involves morality and high ethical standards. We must infuse our values into our work. Work done the right way reflects the ideals and likeness of God. These three dimensions speak to our *posture*, *presentation*, and *perfection*.

BE GLORIFIED

Posture. Glorifying God entails showing reverence for work. This is practically accomplished by maintaining the proper posture.

The posture I am referring to relates to your mental position as opposed to your physical position. Your posture is indicative of the regard you have for your work. I offer three prospective ways you can demonstrate reverence for your work. The first demonstration of reverence is punctuality. This means being on time for work and completing assignments in a timely fashion. While punctuality is admittedly more of a value in Western business contexts, using your time well exhibits reverence for your work in a broader sense. The second demonstration of reverence is dependability. Your work ethic should be beyond reproach. Endeavor to be fair in all of your dealings and trustworthy with respect to your commit-ments. The third demonstration of reverence is integrity. You must always give your full effort regardless of the assignment. The nature of the worker—not the nature of the assignment—renders the work honorable. When you posture yourself in this manner God is glorified through your work.

Presentation. Glorifying God entails showing gratitude for the opportunity to work. You accomplish this practically by presenting yourself in the proper manner. Your talent, ability, and even your life are God-given gifts. Think of these as gifts you can give to others. Offering your God-given gifts in service of others is the first demonstration of gratitude. Your life is a gift that continually gives. Seasoning your words with grace is the second demonstration of gratitude. Be winsome in your communications and use your words to affirm coworkers, customers, and vendors. "Thank you" is a simple yet effective way to show gratitude. The third demon-stration is being generous with your time, talent, and treasure. Your talent can be applied to your primary vocation as well as volunteer opportunities. The money you earn can also be used to support good causes. When you present yourself in a manner that expresses appreciation, God is glorified through your work.

Perfection. Glorifying God entails modeling excellence in the workplace. This is practically accomplished by perfecting your craft. Glorifying God requires you to hold yourself to the highest professional and ethical standards. With respect to your occupation, your objective is to excel at whatever you do. Therefore, the first demonstration of excellence is to exceed the expectations of the beneficiaries of your work. Exceeding the expectations of your customers, coworkers, and employer produces a living example. The second demonstration of excellence relates to perfecting your character. Treating others with care and respect models mature behavior. Being transparent and humble in your dealings enables others to see your perfecting process and helps others pursue excellence of character. The final demonstration of excellence involves exerting positive influence on the work environment. By bringing about improvements in productivity, policies, or procedures you can positively impact the workplace.

Perfecting your work in these ways glorifies God. It is important to note that this extends beyond individual practice. Increasingly organizations are putting more emphasis on corporate social responsibility. Glorifying God extends to the entities to which we devote our time and talent. This is reflected by emphasizing ethical behavior in the workplace, which includes offering all workers fair compensation and protecting workers from harassment. It extends to our engagement in the communities in which we do business. It is not simply relegated to how we treat customers but also how we treat the poor and marginalized. It is reflected by committing to sustainable practices that preserve natural resources and protect the environment. Our work in the earth resounds to the heavens when we serve the common good.

THE BEAUTIFUL ONES

Agnes Bojaxhiu was born in the Republic of Macedonia.[2] During her adolescent years she began to pursue a religious life including pilgrimages to the shrine to pray. She was influenced by stories about the lives of missionaries. At the age of eighteen, she left her family and homeland to join a convent in Ireland. There she would learn English and afterwards, spend nearly two decades serving at a convent in India. While serving at the convent, her attention was constantly drawn to the impoverished people of Calcutta. After seventeen years of teaching at the convent school, she felt a fresh vocational calling. She said she heard a voice from God calling on her to serve the poorest of the poor. Her new mission would be to serve the poor while living among them. She knew this was the vocation for which she was called from her youth. Upon taking her vows to become a nun, she chose the name Teresa in honor of the Patron Saint of missionaries. This was especially fitting given what was revealed with regard to the next chapter of her work life. She displayed an extraordinary commitment to the hungry, crippled, and destitute. Her unique calling to serve those who are ordinarily shunned by society has inspired millions. The world came to know Agnes as Saint Teresa of Calcutta, and more commonly, Mother Teresa.

Few people experience the clarity of vocational calling Mother Teresa exhibited. Far fewer would sacrifice all of their time, talent, and substance for little in the form of material gain. However, this small woman from Albania adopted a land foreign to her and went about serving the poorest members of society. When Mother Teresa began her work, she had no funding and no source of income. She literally took a leap of faith and had to beg for food and supplies. She intimately experienced the life circumstances of those she served. Despite the personal challenges, she was wholly committed to her work. She subsequently founded the Missionaries of Charity, an organization that grew to over four thousand missionaries who managed orphanages, hospices, shelters, and schools. Mother Teresa was very wise. She understood individuals with the noblest intentions fail to find fulfillment in work and life. She thus encouraged people to discover the calling within their vocational calling.

Mother Teresa's testimony serves as a guidepost as we seek to discover joy in our work. One of the more instructive insights I find from her example is we must not stop short in our search or discovery process. Finding work well-aligned with our interest and abilities is beneficial. That alone will not unlock our full potential and reveal our deepest joy. "There is always the danger that we may just do the work for the sake of the work," Mother Teresa warned.[3] In my vocational pursuits, I have experienced the dangers that cause us to miss the calling within our calling. Prideful ambition and selfish gain are always near as we pursue success in our work. Mother Teresa rightly encourages us to seek the greater purpose of our work. I have found the greater purpose is always greater than my personal ambition and far greater than my limited imagination. The greater purpose always positively impacts others and makes the work more meaningful. This leads to Mother Teresa's encouragement that we glorify God through our work. "This is where the respect and the love and the devotion come in—that we do it to God, to Christ, and that's why we try to do it as beautifully as possible."[4] When we commit our work to God, it is a beautiful sight for the world to see.

Mother Teresa's words echo the counsel I received from my mother as I have explored my vocational interests. Their examples combine to teach us an essential lesson. When you discover the calling within the calling, your life's work glorifies God. Mothers are the beautiful ones who shine like the North Star. They help us find clarity of purpose in our work and in our lives. These two mothers and countless others are shining examples of what it means to find the calling within the calling. My mother's story is still being written. While working full time, my parents cofounded a church in the inner city. Though she has retired from her social services occupation, she is very actively working. For nearly twenty-five years, my parents have served their congregation and local community. Their workdays don't have discernible boundaries. They serve when, where, and as they are able and needed. What I find most remarkable about the work they do is that they have never accepted a salary. They view their work in accordance with a greater purpose, and they have a joy money can't provide. I better understand my mother's commitment to glorify God through her work. My parents are shining examples for others. They are beautiful ones.

I offer a final word of encouragement as it concerns your vocational calling. The examples I have cited are indeed examples. You and I can similarly serve as examples, discovering joy in work in the process. Moreover, God's grace is fully available to us all. If we look closely, we see the manifestation of grace in our personal journeys. The ability to experience joy in your work is not a function of the work you do. Your joy comes as a result of the application of the principles we have explored. When you find joy in your work you will be energized because you derive deeper fulfillment from it. The meaningfulness causes you to feel you are the "right person" for the job. In other words, it feels like a good fit for who you are. It aligns with your values and comes naturally to you. The greatest attainment of joy comes from the alignment of your work with your ability, values, and calling.

Whatever your task, big or small, be the right person for the job and commit your work to God. When you adopt this attitude toward your vocation, you are truly doing God's work. The best of who you are can be revealed through your work, and the best of who God is can be revealed through you. And the world will see you, too, are one of the beautiful ones.

Work Glorifies God

KEY INSIGHTS

- Honor God by demonstrating a high regard for every aspect of your work. This requires clarity of purpose, maturity of character, and excellence of achievement.

- The ability to pursue meaningful work is a blessing. Your work provides the opportunity to show your appreciation and the means to pay your gratitude forward.

- Infuse your values—morality and high ethical standards—into your work.

- Qualities such as punctuality, consistency, diligence, and reliability demonstrate reverence for your work.

- Offer your God-given gifts in service of others being generous with your time, talent, and treasure.

- Treating others with care and respect allows you to exert positive influence on your work environment and to serve as a living example.

- When you discover the calling within the calling, your life's work glorifies God.

EPILOGUE

JOY TO THE WORLD

*A person can do nothing better than to eat
and drink and find satisfaction in their own work.
This too, I see, is from the hand of God.*

KING SOLOMON

My office building recently underwent notable renovations to enhance the aesthetics and tenant experience. A very noticeable part of the modernization was the addition of high definition display monitors in the lobby and the elevators. Inasmuch as the expected elevator ride time is short, the displays offer snack-size content such as news briefs, sports scores, and survey results. A recent finding from a survey sponsored by the Faas Foundation caught my attention.[1] The overwhelming majority of the workers surveyed said they are unhappy with their current jobs. And they were not idly standing by, given that 71 percent were actively seeking a change of employment.

While the implications of the survey are debatable, the general findings are uncontroversial. We know through practical experience many individuals are unhappy with their work and their work environment. We know others have yet to discover the fulfillment meaningful work offers. And we personally know individuals seeking joy in their work on a more continuous basis. I understand this in a deeply personal way because at various times I have been the person in question. I suspect this has been the case for you as well.

Let's consider the same survey findings from a different lens. A subset of the workers surveyed bucked the prevailing trend. It is reasonable to assume many from this cohort are not just satisfied but enjoy their work and their work environment. They represent living testimonies of individuals who have discovered joy in their work. For some, it may be a function of a good match between their passion and their profession. For others, they may thrive in their work environment and enjoy being around their coworkers. Of course, for some both may be true. How have they found this level of fulfillment and what does it portend for us? I believe they have achieved this condition through a purposeful search. I believe this because I have seen real life examples. I also know this through my personal journey of discovering joy in my work.

THE SEED, THE SOIL, AND THE SEASON

When we moved into our current home, a portion of our yard was fairly barren. I prefer a plush green yard, so I made a Saturday morning pilgrimage to the local home improvement store. The solution seemed easy enough. My mission was to purchase grass seed. I envisioned my lawn being nurtured to pristine condition in no time. I proceeded directly to the lawn and garden section and grabbed a bag of seed. I figured there was no need to consult the staff, as I trusted my purchase of a recognizable brand. Besides, I had taken a similar tact at our previous home with little challenge. Unfortunately, prior experience does not predict future performance. After weeks of watering and waiting, no new grass had sprung forth. Needless to say, I was dissatisfied with the results.

I decided to return to the same store during the fall to purchase a superior product. A pleasant associate working in the home and garden department greeted me. I disclosed my unsuccessful effort and asked if he might offer some advice regarding my next purchase. He asked me three simple questions. What type of seed had I used previously? What was the condition of the soil? What time of year had I planted the seeds? I recalled purchasing a product touted as a "quick-fix" mix. I wanted to improve my lawn as quickly as possible. As far as the soil condition, I noted the area was arid and dry. The location did not have shrubbery or tree cover and received limited shade during the day. I had seeded the area eight weeks prior during the summer month of July. He told me he understood why my prior attempt was unsuccessful and assured me he could help me achieve a better outcome.

He began by addressing the seed. The grass seed I selected was most suitable for cool, moist conditions. Conversely, I was seeding a sunbaked area in dry conditions. He said it was possible to seed an area in the late summer. I simply hadn't selected the proper product. This was more an issue of fit and had nothing to do with the quality of the seed. He advised me it was best to use cool weather seed in early fall and warm weather seed in spring and summer. Next, he addressed the soil. The arid condition of the topsoil was likely not conducive to a fresh planting. Seeds perform best when they are sown into fertile topsoil with a high concentration of minerals and water. He advised me to prepare the area with fresh topsoil or to consider a mixture that includes seed and mulch to repair the area. The seeds require a fertile environment to flourish. Finally, he addressed the timing. While grass can be planted at various times during the year, the choice of season matters. Given my unique circumstances, he advised me to wait until early spring. I heeded his advice and experienced a completely different outcome the following spring. The lesson is this: you have to plant the right seed, in the right soil, during the right season.

How does this apply to discovering joy in your work? Think of the seed as the time, talent, and treasure you devote to your vocation and life's work. In a more profound way, think of the seed as your soul. Discovering joy in your work only occurs by means of self-discovery. By transforming your occupation into your vocation, you develop into the type of individual who can find measures of success and fulfillment in any type of work. Think of the soil as your work conditions. Seek a work environment that best aligns with your skills, interests, and values. This is enabled through self-awareness and wise counsel. Your external environment is not the only condition that matters. Your internal condition, or the attitude of your heart, is what matters most. Cultivate the soil of your heart to ensure you flourish in your work. This involves breaking down mental barriers and overcoming unhealthy perceptions. It also involves filling your mind and heart with productive thoughts and ideas. Finally, consider the season. Remember, bloom where you are planted. You must realize different seeds bloom in different seasons. Understanding your purpose allows your work to exhibit patience. Patience is the proverbial living water that refreshes your soul at work. This perfecting patience allows grace and timing to work on your behalf. Sowing your seed in the proper season helps you along the path to discovering joy in your work.

THESE THREE WORDS

Let's revisit the three essential terms from the introduction. *Work* is the first essential term and is the principal focus of the book. Work is physical or mental effort applied to achieve intended results. Your work is a vital part of your life to which you devote significant time and energy. Your work entails much more than the wages you earn. The opportunity to work is one of life's greatest gifts, providing you with immeasurable worth when you pursue it properly. You engage in meaningful work through your primary occupation, secondary vocation, and volunteer activities. This work is generally done in partnership as part of a shared vision and mission. Work is not synonymous with activity or busyness. Your work is intended to produce lasting value and should always be purposeful and productive.

Joy is the second essential term. Work is intended to be meaningful, and finding meaning in your work gives you joy. Joy is a source of great pleasure that results from the discovery of something especially good. While joy is reflected by your emotions, it is more than a happy feeling. Joy emanates from your internal condition as opposed to your external circumstances. You can experience joy in any type of work. You must, however, adopt the right mindset. A healthy attitude toward your work and your workplace is only attained through intentional effort. The essential truths, valuable insights, and practical applications we explored illuminate the path to discovering joy in our work.

Transform is the third and final term. In this context, the term refers to your advancement or development. You are responsible for the quality of your work experience. Discovering joy in your work begins with self-awareness. You can best pursue your vocation when you know yourself. Knowing yourself involves recognizing your unique personality, innate abilities, and deepest passions. Careful introspection produces a healthy self-image. Introspection also produces a healthy attitude toward those you work with. In this way, your work reflects the best of who you are yet does not define your self-worth. This kind of selflessness makes your work more enjoyable. Albeit personal, the admonishment of transformation is far from a selfish endeavor. Indeed, you will need coworkers and mentors to aid you in the process. Your life is an unending journey toward becoming your best self. With self-awareness as your precursor, you must progress to self-development. Specifically, you must develop your character to fulfill your potential. This involves altering your expectations and behaviors.

Your work aids you in your maturation process. Your ultimate objective is to mature professionally and personally. This perfecting process is the key to discovering the path to joy in your work and in your life.

WORDS TO THE WISE

A creed is a set of beliefs or aims. The term is historically associated with formal statements or systems of religious belief. I recently viewed a program where the interviewer highlighted the police officer's creed. It reads, in part, "As a law enforcement officer, my fundamental duty is to serve mankind; to safeguard lives and property, to protect the innocent against deception, the weak against oppression and intimidation, and the peaceful against violence and disorder; and to respect the constitutional rights of all men to liberty, equality, and justice." This is a remarkable statement of belief. It reflects the reality that law enforcement officers regularly risk their lives to uphold their beliefs and serve others.

Derrick, a seasoned law enforcement officer, is one of these brave souls. Over the course of his career, Derrick has worked on a wide variety of assignments including patrol, narcotics, domestic violence, sexual assault, missing persons, and special investigations. While many people willfully turn a blind eye to the injustices that plague our communities, Derrick sees them as a call to action. When I asked Derrick why he became a police officer, he offered the following response. "My original motivation was an interest in doing something professionally that would allow me to be active while having diversity in my daily duties. I quickly realized I had the power to effect change in the community I served."

"So how do you deal with the difficulties of the job and the atrocities you see?" I asked.

"Law enforcement is complex. While my experience has been honorable, many people have unfavorable views of police officers. We are often judged as a collective group rather than on individual merit. This is by far the most difficult part of the job. The one constant that provides satisfaction is protecting the innocent and holding wrongdoers accountable for their actions. This is the most enjoyable part of my work and it gives me a sense of fulfilment."

The law officer's creed represents more than mere words to Derrick. It reflects his personal beliefs, which have allowed him to transform an honorable occupation into a lifelong vocation. Our lives are safer and richer because of countless men and women like Derrick who are called to protect and serve.

Wise King Solomon offers us timeless words of working wisdom. "A person can do nothing better than to eat and drink and find satisfaction in their own toil [work]. This too, I see, is from the hand of God" (Eccles 2:24). Solomon's observation offers four revelatory insights. First, he asserts there is nothing better than finding fulfillment in your work. While this is not an absolute statement, it clearly sets this discovery apart as immensely rewarding. Discovering joy in your work is one of the most valuable pursuits life has to offer. Second, he uses the term *find*, which affirms it is only obtained by virtue of a purposeful effort. Third, he refers to your own work. In the journey of life, you must run your own race. Your path is unique and your choice of vocation is separate and distinct from all other persons. Finally, he observes, joyful work is a godsend. It is a divine blessing, which is part of your greater purpose.

Sowing the right seed, in the right soil, in the right season allows you to flourish. When you develop the proper character traits, cultivate the proper attitude, and align your work with your purpose, you are destined to flourish in work and in life. This working wisdom leads to the path of discovering joy in your work. May your work, joy, and life be full.

ACKNOWLEDGMENTS

My coworkers, my mentors, my friends, my parents, my children, my wife, and my Creator.

NOTES

INTRODUCTION

[1] AnnaMarie Mann, Jim Harter, "The Worldwide Employee Engagement Crisis," Gallup Workplace, January 7, 2016, www.gallup.com/work place/236495/worldwide-employee-engagement-crisis.aspx.

[2] Henri J.M. Nouwen, *Can You Drink the Cup?* (Notre Dame, IN: Ave Maria Press, 1996), 26-27.

[3] Joseph Hartropp, "'Joy Is the Simplest Form of Gratitude': 12 Quotes from Legendary Theologian Karl Barth," *Christian Today*, May 10, 2017, www .christiantoday.com/article/joy-is-the-simplest-form-of-gratitude-12-quotes -from-legendary-theologian-karl-barth/108806.htm.

[4] Goldie Hawn with Wendy Holden, *A Lotus Grows in the Mud* (New York: Putnam, 2005), 17.

PART ONE: YOUR WORKPLACE

[1] Rudyard Kipling, "If—," PoetryFoundation.org (1943, *A Choice of Kipling's Verse*), accessed February 18, 2019, www.poetryfoundation.org/poems/46473 /if---.

1 CHANGE YOUR ATTITUDE

[1] Michelle Hackman and Eric Morath, "Teachers Quit Jobs at the Highest Rate on Record," *The Wall Street Journal*, December 28, 2018, www.wsj.com /articles/teachers-quit-jobs-at-highest-rate-on-record-11545993052.

2 ALTER YOUR APPROACH

[1] William Ernest Henley, "Invictus," PoetryFoundation.org, accessed February 18, 2019, www.poetryfoundation.org/poems/51642/invictus.

[2] Europeana Blog, "Icon of Expression: Vincent van Gogh," March 30, 2012, blog.europeana.eu/2012/03/icon-of-expression-vincent-van-gogh/.

[3] Stephen R. Covey, A. Roger Merrill, and Rebecca R. Merrill, *First Things First* (New York: Fireside, 1994).

3 RAISE YOUR APTITUDE

[1]ManpowerGroup, *2015 Talent Shortage Survey*, (Milwaukee, WI: Manpower-Group, 2015): 2, www.manpowergroup.com/wps/wcm/connect/db23c560 -08b6-485f-9bf6-f5f38a43c76a/2015_Talent_Shortage_Survey_US-lo_res .pdf?MOD=AJPERES.

[2]Martin Luther King Jr., "What Is Your Life's Blueprint?" speech, Barratt Junior High School, Philadelphia, PA, transcript, www.drmartinluther kingjr.com/whatisyourlifesblueprint.htm.

[3]See www.keirsey.com.

[4]See www.gallupstrengthscenter.com/home/en-us/strengthsfinder.

[5]See www.kolbe.com/assessments.

[6]King, "What Is Your Life's Blueprint?"

4 ENSURE YOUR ACHIEVEMENT

[1]Cheryl Conner, "Wasting Time at Work: The Epidemic Continues," *Forbes*, July 31, 2015, www.forbes.com/sites/cherylsnappconner/2015/07/31 /wasting-time-at-work-the-epidemic-continues/#3f9afb591d94.

[2]CareerBuilder, "New CareerBuilder Survey Reveals How Much Smart-phones Are Sapping Productivity at Work," June 9, 2016, www.career builder.com/share/aboutus/pressreleasesdetail.aspx?sd=6%2f9%2f2016&site id=cbpr&sc_cmp1=cb_pr954_&id=pr954&ed=12%2f31%2f2016.

[3]Salary.com Staff, "Why & How Your Employees Are Wasting Time at Work," April 17, 2018, www.salary.com/articles/why-how-your-employees -are-wasting-time-at-work/.

[4]Carol W. Gelderman, "Henry Ford," Encyclopaedia Britannica, last updated January 28, 2019, www.britannica.com/biography/Henry-Ford.

5 FOR THE LOVE OF MONEY

[1]Sam Polk, "For the Love of Money," *The New York Times*, January 18, 2014, www.nytimes.com/2014/01/19/opinion/sunday/for-the-love-of-money.html.

[2]Dan Ariely, "What Makes Us Feel Good About Our Work?" (TEDx-RiodelaPlata, October, 2012), www.ted.com/talks/dan_ariely_what_makes _us_feel_good_about_our_work.

[3]"What is Net Worth?" Investopedia Video Definitions, last updated No-vember 26, 2018, www.investopedia.com/video/play/what-net-worth/.

[4]The O'Jays, "For the Love of Money," Kenneth Gamble, Leon Huff, and Anthony Jackson, recorded October 3, 1973, track 5 on *Ships Ahoy*,

Philadelphia International Records, 45 rpm. See also www.youtube.com
/watch?v=GXE_n2q08Yw.

[5]From an interview in 1905. Peter Collier and David Horowitz, *The Rockefellers,
an American Dynasty* (New York: Holt, Rinehart & Winston, 1976), 48.

6 FOR THE PRAISE OF PEOPLE

[1]*Encyclopaedia Britannica Online*, "Carl Phillip Emanuel Bach," last mod-
ified March 22, 2007, www.britannica.com/biography/Carl-Philipp
-Emanuel-Bach.

[2]Howard Chandler Robbins Landon, *Haydn, A Documentary Study* (London:
Thames & Hudson Ltd., 1981), 88.

7 FOR THE PRIDE OF LIFE

[1]Josh Jones, "How Aretha Franklin Turned Otis Redding's 'Respect' Into a
Civil Rights and Feminist Anthem," *Open Culture*, August 20, 2018, www
.openculture.com/2018/08/aretha-franklin-turned-otis-reddings-respect
-civil-rights-feminist-anthem.html.

[2]Encyclopedia.com, "Kaiser, Henry," accessed February 12, 2019, www.en
cyclopedia.com/people/social-sciences-and-law/business-leaders/henry
-john-kaiser.

[3]Martin Luther King Jr., "Loving Your Enemies," Sermon Delivered at Dexter
Avenue Baptist Church, November 17, 1957, Montgomery, AL, kinginstitute
.stanford.edu/king-papers/documents/loving-your-enemies-sermon
-delivered-dexter-avenue-baptist-church.

PART THREE: YOUR WORK LIFE

[1]James Hamblin, "Why Succeeding Against the Odds Can Make You Sick,"
The New York Times, January 27, 2017, Opinion, www.nytimes.com
/2017/01/27/opinion/sunday/why-succeeding-against-the-odds-can-make
-you-sick.html.

[2]Carlene Hempel, "The Man—Facts, Fiction, and Themes," John Henry, The
Steel Driving Man, December 1998, www.ibiblio.org/john_henry/analysis.html.

[3]Stanford University Communications, "'You've Got to Find What You Love,'
Jobs Says," June 14, 2015, news.stanford.edu/2005/06/14/jobs-061505/.

[4]Stanford, "You've Got to Find What You Love."

8 WORK REVEALS PURPOSE

[1]Carol Hymowitz, "Me, Retire? Settling into a Life of Leisure Is Becoming the Exception," *Bloomberg BusinessWeek*, September 29, 2017.

[2]Dyfed Loesche, "How Americans Commute to Work," *Statista*, October 5, 2017, www.statista.com/chart/11355/how-americans-commute-to-work/.

[3]Annemarie Schimmel, "Rumi," *Encyclopaedia Britannica Online*, April 6, 2017, www.britannica.com/biography/Rumi.

[4]Mihaly Csikszentmihyi, *Flow: The Psychology of Optimal Experience* (1990; New York: Harper Perennial Modern Classics, 2008).

9 WORK REQUIRES EFFORT

[1]Will Durant, *The Story of Philosophy* (1926; New York: Simon & Schuster, 2005), 61.

11 WORK DEVELOPS SKILL

[1]Thomas Davidson to the class in history and social science in the Educational Alliance, New York, NY, May 31, 1899, in *The Education of the Wage-Earners*, ed. Charles M. Blakewell (1904; Collingwood, Victoria: Trieste Publishing, 2018), Chapter V.

12 WORK FOSTERS RELATIONSHIPS

[1]Paul J. Zak, "The Neuroscience of Trust," *Harvard Business Review* (January–February 2017), hbr.org/2017/01/the-neuroscience-of-trust.

[2]See www.mattieonline.com.

[3]These stages of a group were first identified and named by psychologist Bruce Tuckman in a 1965 article. See Mind Tools Content Team, "Forming, Storming, Norming, and Performing: Understanding the Stages of Team Formation," Mind Tools, accessed February 18, 2019, www.mindtools.com/pages/article/newLDR_86.htm.

[4]Brian Tracy, "The Power of Positive Thinking: How Thoughts Can Change Your Life," Brian Tracy International Blog, accessed February 12, 2019, www.briantracy.com/blog/personal-success/positive-attitude-happy-people-positive-thinking/.

[5]"About Scott Adams," Scott Adams' Blog, accessed February 12, 2019, blog.dilbert.com/about/.

[6]Scott Adams, "Culture as Asset," *Dilbert*, April 26, 2017, dilbert.com/strip/2017-04-26.

13 WORK PRODUCES VALUE

[1]Theodore Roosevelt, *Theodore Roosevelt: An Autobiography* (1913; Project Gutenberg, 2006), www.gutenberg.org/files/3335/3335-h/3335-h.htm.

[2]Mind Tools Content Team, "SMART Goals: How to Make Your Goals Achievable," Mind Tools, accessed February 12, 2019, www.mindtools.com /pages/article/smart-goals.htm.

[3]History.com editors, "Theodore Roosevelt," History.com, last updated September 19, 2018, www.history.com/topics/us-presidents/theodore-roosevelt.

14 WORK GLORIFIES GOD

[1]See www.fmsc.org.

[2]Biography.com editors, "Mother Teresa Biography," Biography.com, last updated January 17, 2018, www.biography.com/people/mother-teresa-9504160.

[3]Mother Teresa in *The Joy in Loving*, ed. Jaya Chaliha and Edward Le Joly (New York: Viking Penguin, 1996), 138.

[4]Mother Teresa in Malcom Muggeridge, *Something Beautiful for God* (New York: Harper & Row, 1986), 15.

EPILOGUE: JOY TO THE WORLD

[1]Carmine Gallo, "A New Study Finds Most Employees Want to Quit, But There's a Simple Way to Keep Them Happy," *Forbes*, October 25, 2017, www.forbes.com/sites/carminegallo/2017/10/25/a-new-study-finds-most -employees-want-to-quit-but-theres-a-simple-way-to-keep-them-happy.

ABOUT THE AUTHOR

S hundrawn A. Thomas is a gifted writer, teacher, and executive. Professionally, he serves as president of a trillion-dollar global investment management business and is a management group member of a leading financial services company. He previously advised institutional equity investors as a vice president for Goldman Sachs, and held positions in sales, trading, and research in the fixed income division of Morgan Stanley. He holds a BS in accounting from Florida A&M University and an MBA from the University of Chicago Booth School of Business. Shundrawn is widely respected by professional colleagues for his dedication to excellence and principled business approach. His industry leadership includes serving on the Board of Governors for the Investment Company Institute and other industry associations.

Shundrawn is a motivational speaker and lecturer speaking nationally on topics including professional development, leadership, values, faith, strategy, and finance. He is an engaged civic leader serving as a trustee for Wheaton College and as a board director of the Museum of Science and Industry. Shundrawn serves his local community as assistant pastor of Look Up and Live Full Gospel Ministries located on Chicago's Southside. Shundrawn is happily married and has two sons. In his personal time, he enjoys reading, running, and traveling. He is the author of *Ridiculous Faith: Ordinary People Living Extraordinary Lives* and *Driving Under the Influence: Finding Your Way on the Road of Life*.